OSPREY AIRCRAFT OF THE ACES® • 58

Slovakian and Bulgarian Aces of World War 2

SERIES EDITOR: TONY HOLMES

OSPREY AIRCRAFT OF THE ACES® • 58

Slovakian and Bulgarian Aces of World War 2

Jiri Rajlich, Stephan Boshniakov
and Petko Mandjukov

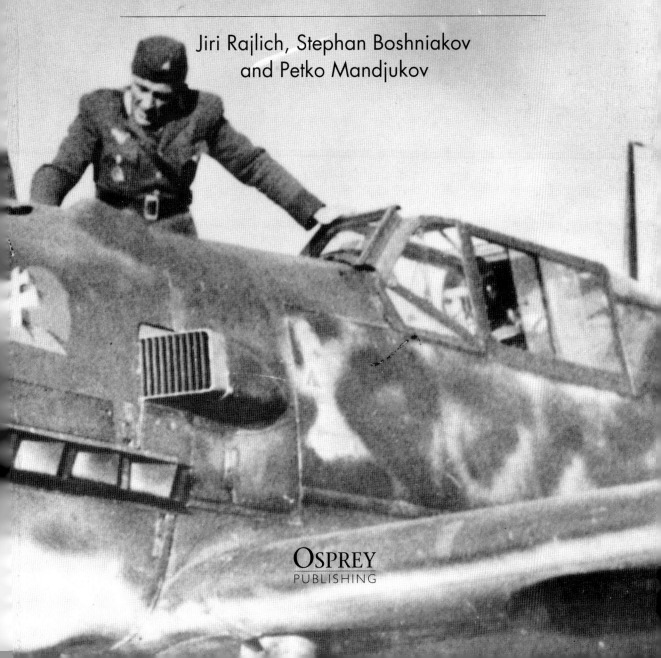

OSPREY
PUBLISHING

Front Cover
On the morning of 28 November 1942, members of 13(*slow*)./JG 52 encountered Soviet fighters for the first time. During a *freie Jagd* near Tuapse, in the Caucasus, two Slovak Bf 109E-7s, piloted by porucik (second lieutenant) Vladimir Krisko and catnik (sergeant) Jozef Jancovic, met nine Soviet Polikarpov I-153 Chaika biplanes. After a short fight, three kills were claimed by the Slovaks, the first by Krisko in Bf 109E-7 Wk-Nr 6474 White 12 and the other two by Jancovic. However, due to the rigorous German checking procedure, none of these kills was officially confirmed.

After scoring seven confirmed victories, 'Jozo' Jancovic was fatally wounded while flying Bf 109G-2 Wk-Nr 14380 in combat with LaGG-3 fighters over the south coast of the Sea of Azov on 29 March 1943. He crash-landed near the village of Akhtanizovskaya, but died the next day. Between February and July 1943, 'Vlado' Krisko shot down nine Soviet aircraft. One year later he took an active part in the anti-Nazi uprising in Slovakia and survived the war (*Cover artwork by Mark Postlethwaite*)

First published in Great Britain in 2004 by Osprey Publishing
Elms Court, Chapel Way, Botley, Oxford, OX2 9LP

ISBN 1 84176 652 6

Edited by Tony Holmes and Bruce Hales-Dutton
Page design by Mark Holt
Cover Artwork by Mark Postlethwaite
Aircraft Profiles by John Weal
Index by Alan Thatcher
Origination by Grasmere Digital Imaging, Leeds, UK
Printed in China through Bookbuilders

04 05 06 07 08   10 9 8 7 6 5 4 3 2 1

ACKNOWLEDGEMENTS
Jiri Rajlich wishes to thank the following individuals for their invaluable help – Stefan Androvic, Bernd Barbas, Winfried Bock, the late Rudolf Bozik, Frantisek Cyprich, Anton Droppa, Martin Fekets, the late Werner Girbig, Frantisek Hanovec, Jaroslav Janecka, Vladimir Karlicky, Milan Krajci, the late Juraj Rajninec, Jan Reznak, Jiri Sehnal, the late Stanislav Spurny and Ladislav Valousek.

EDITOR'S NOTE
To make this best-selling series as authoritative as possible, the Editor would be interested in hearing from any individual who may have relevant photographs, documentation or first-hand experiences relating to the world's elite pilots, and their aircraft, of the various theatres of war. Any material used will be credited to its original source. Please contact Tony Holmes via e-mail at: tony.holmes@osprey-jets.freeserve.co.uk

For details of all Osprey Publishing titles please contact us at:

Osprey Direct UK, P.O. Box 140, Wellingborough, Northants NN8 2FA, UK
E-mail: **info@ospreydirect.co.uk**

Osprey Direct USA, c/o MBI Publishing, P.O. Box 1, 729 Prospect Ave, Osceola, WI 54020, USA
E-mail: **info@ospreydirectusa.com**

Or visit our website: **www.ospreypublishing.com**

CONTENTS

INTRODUCTION

Like the Serbs and Croats, the Czechs and Slovaks share a similar language but have a different history – political, constitutional, economic and cultural. Until the foundation of the Czechoslovak Republic in October 1918, they were separate nations, the Czechs in the Austrian part and the Slovaks in the Hungarian area of the Habsburg empire. The Czechs had maintained an independent kingdom until the 17th century and played an important role in Europe, but the Slovaks were subject to long-term rule by Hungary.

This represented a systematic attempt to extinguish Slovakian independence, and without the existence of Czechoslovakia, there was a danger of its extinction as a nation. While the territory of the former Bohemian kingdom, formed by Bohemia, Moravia and Silesia, was the most highly-developed and industrial part of the Habsburg empire, Slovakia's economy was an almost exclusively backward and agricultural one. Unlike the more liberal-minded Czechs who were comparatively cool towards religious matters, the conservative Slovaks maintained a strong Catholic tradition.

Between the wars Czechoslovakia comprised Bohemia, Moravia, Silesia, Slovakia and Ruthenia. It was a fairly well-developed and liberal democratic state whose foreign policy was aligned towards France, the nation which was the chief guarantor of its independence. As with other Central and East European states, Czechoslovakia was a mix of different nationalities.

In 1921 there were 13.6 million inhabitants, of which 6.8 million were Czechs (51 per cent) and 1.9 million Slovaks (14.5 per cent). Officially, both groups were Czechoslovaks and formed two-thirds of the population. The remaining third comprised 3.1 million Germans (23.4 per cent), 745,000 Hungarians (5.4 per cent), 461,000 Ruthenians (3.3 per cent), 180,000 Jews (1.3 per cent) and 75,000 Poles (0.5 per cent). Although these minorities were guaranteed rights in the liberal-oriented Czechoslovakia, many Germans, Hungarians and Poles did not identify themselves with the new state and agitated to join Germany, Hungary and Poland. On top of this, the Czechs and Slovaks were far from being united.

It was these national minorities which played a crucial role in the break-up of Czechoslovakia during the crisis which led to the Munich Treaty in September 1938, when France and Britain hoped to maintain peace in Europe. However, only the autocratic regimes of the three neighbouring states derived any advantage from the situation. France and Britain lost a trading partner and a strong ally in Central Europe as a consequence.

Under pressure from four European powers, Czechoslovakia had to cede vast border territories (improperly called *Sudetenland*, and inhabited by 2.8 million Germans and 727,000 Czechs) to neighbouring Nazi Germany. Poland gained disputed smaller areas in the north of Moravia (Tesin) and Slovakia (Orava and Spis) inhabited by 66,000 Poles, 120,000 Czechs and Slovaks and 16,000 Germans. Hungary claimed its portion of the booty in November 1938 in the form of the long-coveted so-called *Felvidek* (Upper Country), together with large areas of southern Slovakia and Ruthenia. With the Hungarian occupation came 972,000 inhabitants

– 524,000 Hungarians, 300,000 Slovaks, 40,000 Ruthenians, 50,000 Jews and 10,000 Germans.

The Czechoslovak state had not only lost 30 per cent of its territory and 34 per cent of its total population, but also a large part of its industrial and agricultural potential, to say nothing of its defensive positions. A crippled and non-viable state was now left wide open to its aggressive neighbours.

The final act of the drama was played out in March 1939. First, Hitler gave support to Slovak separatists by giving them an ultimatum to break away from the Czech rump. On the 14th the Slovak state was proclaimed in what had until then been provincial Bratislava. It had now become a true vassal of Nazi Germany. After brutal diplomatic and military pressure Germany, occupied the remaining Czech territory the next day.

The swastika flew over the once proud and historic city of Prague, and the following day the Protectorate Bohemia and Moravia was proclaimed under the protection of the Third Reich. Czechoslovakia ceased to exist, vanishing from the political map of Europe for several years.

The two nations drifted apart. During the next six years, graduates from the sole pre-war Czechoslovak pilots' school were to wear the uniforms of five different air forces. The combined total of kills they scored numbered 525 aircraft, displaying not only German, Italian and Hungarian markings, but also those of Poland, the USSR and the USA. There was not much amity left, and the Czechs and Slovaks fought each other.

Czechoslovaks – that is Czechs and some 'Czechoslovak'-oriented Slovaks – defected to Poland, France, Britain and the USSR to fight against Germany. Fighting for the Allies, they downed 304 aircraft confirmed (and another 83 probables) and produced 29 aces, the best known being Karel Kuttelwascher, Josef Frantisek and Alois Vasatko.

Things were different in Slovakia. In March 1939 it was forced to defend its newly-proclaimed independence in a border conflict with Hungary. But there were already doubts about this neo-fascist state. On 23 March 1939 the so-called Protection Pact with Nazi Germany was signed in Vienna. Without waiting for it to be ratified, the *Wehrmacht* marched into the so-called Protective Zone in West Slovakia and annexed all military facilities in the region, including the airfields at Zilina and Malacky-Novy Dvor.

Formed under the 'protection' of the *Deutsche Luftwaffenmission in der Slowakei*, the Slovak Air Force (officially Slovak Air Arms, or the *Slovenske vzdusne zbrane* – SVZ – from 3 May 1940) fought throughout the war. On 1 September 1939 Slovakia was the only Nazi ally to attack Poland, and on 22 June 1941 it was the first satellite into the USSR.

In December 1941 Slovakia declared war on the USA and Britain, and for this reason it appeared on the list of USAAF bombing targets. Fighting on the Axis side, the so-called 'Tatra Eagles', members of the small SVZ, downed 221 aircraft confirmed (plus another 30 probables). They produced 17 aces, the best-known being Jan Reznak, Izidor Kovarik and Jan Gerthofer. Turning their weapons against the Germans in the summer of 1944, they did their best to earn rehabilitation and reunite the Czechs and Slovaks in the restored state of Czechoslovakia.

BIRTH OF A NATION

Bulgaria emerged from the Ottoman Empire after a war of liberation as an autonomous principality under the sovereignty of the Sultan of Turkey, but with a Christian government. Total independence was declared in 1908. Bulgaria allied itself with Greece, Serbia and Montenegro in order to wrest much of the remaining European territory of the empire from Turkey in the first Balkan war of 1912-13 – a conflict whose savagery and brutality acted as a fitting prelude to World War 1.

Although now a regional superpower whose territory reached the Black Sea, the Sea of Marmara and the Aegean, Bulgaria was dissatisfied with its share of the spoils and went to war with its former allies, provoking intervention from Rumania and Turkey. The resulting treaty stripped Bulgaria of its recently-acquired gains, including Macedonia, and the country entered World War 1 allied to the Central Powers in an attempt to improve its position. In the event Bulgaria was the first of the Central Powers to surrender, in September 1918, having suffered the highest *per capita* loss of all the combatants with over 100,000 killed and 144,000 wounded.

The next few years represented a period of unrest in Bulgaria, characterised by assassination, revolution and terrorism. When Mussolini assumed power in Italy, he made it clear that the Balkans was within the Italian 'sphere of influence'. He offered friendship and co-operation, yet despite *tsar* Boris III's admiration of Mussolini, Bulgaria looked first to Poland and then to Germany to equip its revived air force. Germany sold much equipment stripped from the disbanded Czech air force to Bulgaria at extremely favourable terms, and at the same time Bulgarian officers were sent to Germany for training as fighter pilots and instructors.

In March 1941 Bulgaria joined the Axis Pact, and two days later German troops marched into the country and occupied Black Sea ports. Although Bulgaria played a passive role in Hitler's invasion of Yugoslavia and Greece the following month, its towns were bombed by British and Greek aircraft. Later, Bulgarian troops occupied Yugoslav and Greek Macedonia and parts of Greece itself.

Although the country did not declare war on Britain and the USA until December 1941, Bulgarian aircraft supported German operations in the eastern Mediterranean but reported only two contacts with British submarines. Its fighter force did not enter the war, however, until the USAAF began using Bulgarian airspace for attacks on Rumania and its oilfields. On 14 November 1943, American bombers raided Sofia for the first time. Combat between Bulgarian fighters and US bombers continued into 1944.

In August 1944, with the Red Army approaching, the Bulgarian government changed sides and sought armistice terms from the US and Britain. On 7 September the Soviet army entered Sofia and Bulgaria declared war on Germany. The communists swept away the old system in a series of bloody purges and the air force did not escape these unscathed, for many senior officers were executed. Stripped of their leaders, the Bulgarian armed forces fought on the Soviet side against their former allies partly in the hope that the territories of Macedonia and Thrace could be retained, but this did not happen. About 30,000 Bulgarian service personnel were killed fighting Germany and its remaining allies.

This book tells the story of Slovakian and Bulgarian fighter pilots, and in particular those who were successful enough to become aces. For the first time in the west, the authors tell the stories of these men, aided by extensive research and interviews with surviving participants.

ACES IN AVIAS

Until the Czechoslovak state was dismembered, one of the six air regiments of the Czechoslovak Air Force – the 3rd Air Regiment (*Letecky pluk 3*) – was stationed permanently in Slovakia. From 14 March 1939, it formed the organisational basis of the new Slovak Air Force. At the time there were not more than 230 military aircraft in Slovak territory, 88 of them fighters of which 66 were standard Avia B 534 biplanes, with just 15 of the cannon-armed Bk 534 version. Most belonged to the regiment's five fighter squadrons (*Letka*), with Nos 37, 38, 39 and 45 based at Piestany and No 49 at Spisska Nova Ves (whence No 45 was shortly to be transferred). The remaining seven aircraft were outdated biplane fighters, including two Avia Ba 33s and three B 34s, which were used by the Piestany-based Training and Reserve Squadron.

More serious than the deficiency in equipment was the acute shortage of personnel caused by the departure of Czech pilots and ground specialists to the Protectorate. This left around 80 Slovak pilots and observers, but only six of them had any seniority – one major, two staff captains and three captains.

Yet very early in its life, the newly-formed state had to face an attack by Hungary. After the Czechoslovak Republic split in March 1939, the most easterly part of the country, the economically backward Ruthenia – also known as Sub-Carpathian Ukraine, and attached to Czechoslovakia by an international community of nations in September 1919 – proclaimed its independence. But the Hungarians decided to exploit the situation, and by 17 March had occupied the area. After completely occupying Ruthenia, Hungarian troops crossed the eastern border of Slovakia on the

From 1939 through to 1942, pre-war Avia B 534 biplanes were the standard fighter aircraft of the Slovak Air Arms (*Slovenske vzdusne zbrane*, or SVZ). Pictured here is a Version IV B 534 of No 45 Sqn (*letka 45*) at Spisska Nova Ves aerodrome in March 1939, shortly prior to the conflict with Hungary. At this time Slovak aircraft were still marked with Czechoslovak colours

23rd and began to penetrate further into Slovakia. But the Slovaks resisted and the air force began to play a role in the border conflict.

With its numbers virtually halved by the outflow of Czech personnel, the Slovak Air Force had to face the loss of Kosice and Uzhorod airports due to Vienna arbitrage. In the disputed area of eastern Slovakia, the airfield of Spisska Nova Ves became the main base. Stationed there in March 1939 were two fighter squadrons (Nos 45 and 49) armed with 20 Avia B 534s, together with two reconnaissance squadrons (Nos 12 and 13) equipped with 15 Letov S 328s and five Aero Ap 32s. But even with additional flying personnel drafted in from Piestany and Zilina airfields, these units were still not up to strength.

Although the first reconnaissance flights on 22 March were flown by Slovak pilots, combat missions did not start until the next day when two B 534s were shot down by Hungarian anti-aircraft fire, with another four, plus an S 328, damaged. Fighter pilots porucik Jan Svetlik (CO of No 45 Sqn) and desiatnik Stefan Devan (No 49 Sqn) were the first Slovak airmen to lose their lives in defence of the new state. One pilot was wounded.

The first air battle between Slovak and Hungarian fighters came the following day, and it ended in a decisive victory for the Hungarian Fiat CR.32s of *vadaszszazad* 1/1 *Ijasz* from Uzhorod airfield, in Ruthenia.

At 0740 hrs three No 49 Sqn B 534s, heavily laden with bombs, met an identical number of CR.32s north of Stakcin. The aircraft of unit CO porucik Jan Prhacek was hit by Lt Aladar Negro. Seriously wounded, the Slovak tried to crash-land in the Luhavce Creek valley, but the bombs under the wings of his aircraft exploded and he was killed. Fire from the second Hungarian pilot, Sgt Sandor Szojak, punctured the engine and oil tank of desiatnik Cyril Martis' B 534. He jettisoned his bombs and crash-landed on swampy ground, where the aircraft turned over. Sgt Arpad Kertesz claimed to have downed the third B 534, piloted by slobodnik Michal Karas, near Vysne Remety. In fact Karas made it back to base with his aircraft undamaged. The Hungarians suffered no loss.

At 1000 hrs three No 45 Sqn B 534s took off to bomb tanks near Tibava a Sobrance. Two were downed by Hungarian flak, and although Palenicek managed to crash-land his damaged machine in Slovak-held territory, slobodnik Jozef Zachar was captured, together with his virtually intact B 534.

The biggest battle was fought out during the afternoon of 24 March over Sobrance and Pavlovice na Uhom. A three-aircraft section of No 12 Sqn S 328 reconnaissance machines took-off at 1345 hrs from Spisska Nova Ves to bomb Hungarian units on their way from Uzhorod to Michalovce. They were escorted by three No 45 Sqn B 534s, taking off at 15-minutes intervals, but all three, flown by dostojnicky zastupca Jozef Hergott, catnik Frantisek Hanovec and desiatnik Martin Danihel failed to return.

Strong anti-aircraft fire forced the Slovak group to climb above the clouds, but as soon as they dived they were attacked by nine CR.32s of 1/1 *Ijasz*. Lt Laszlo Palko quickly shot down a Letov, which crashed in flames into a wood near Nizne Remety. Although pilot slobodnik Gustav Pazicky died in the aircraft, observer porucik Ferdinand Svento baled out, his his body riddled with 18 bullet holes. There are differing versions of what had

During its baptism of fire in the conflict with Hungary, the fledgling Slovak Air Force suffered heavy losses. This B 534 was damaged by flak and force-landed in Hungarian-occupied territory on 24 March 1939, its pilot, slobodnik Jozef Zachar, being taken into captivity. He was later repatriated, but his aircraft was not. Instead, it was repaired, repainted with Hungarian camouflage and national insignia (as seen here) and used for tests with the Royal Hungarian Air Force, bearing the fuselage serial G.1+92. Later, it was sent to the aeronautical college at Gyor, where it flew with the civil registration HA-VAB. The machine was finally destroyed at Gyor aerodrome in 1945

happened – Svento was shot by Hungarian soldiers either while he was hanging defenceless in his parachute or after he had reached the ground. The other Letov, piloted by slobodnik Jozef Drlicka, was probably hit in its engine by porucik Matyas Pirity, and it crash-landed near the village of Strazske.

One by one, all three escorting Avias were forced out of the fight. Hergott crash-landed his heavily damaged and burning machine southeast of Banovce nad Ondavou. Danihel, his fuel tank punctured, came down in a field near Brezovice nad Torysou, while Hanovec, the third member of the escorting formation, crashed near Senne at Michalovce. Only the S 328 flown by slobodnik Jan Maco returned to base.

Although actual Slovak losses had totalled two Letovs and three Avias, the Hungarians claimed the Letovs (by Palko and Pirithy) and five Avias (by Lts Aladar Negro, Antal Bekassy, Bela Csemke, the leader of the Hungarian formation, and Sgts Sandor Szojak and Arpad Kertesz). The Hungarians suffered no loss. The Slovak press, however, reported that Danihel and Hanovec – a future ace with five confirmed kills plus one probable – had each shot down a CR.32.

'I was attacked by several enemy aircraft', Hanovec recalled later. 'I got into a big fight and climbed into the clouds. When I got out, I saw my pursuers circling near where I had escaped from them. I opened fire and they swooped on me. One flew towards the nose of my aeroplane. I thought we would collide. At the same time I opened fire. From about 40 m (130 ft) I noticed black smoke coming from the enemy aircraft. I steered away and he flew about 5 m (about 15 ft) over my aeroplane, and I saw he was burning. But I had enough to do to avoid the collision. We only just passed each other – I went up and he went down. I was then fired at by fighters and anti-aircraft guns. My engine was damaged so badly that it cut out and I had to crash-land.'

This photograph was taken at Spisska Nova Ves on 5 March 1940, the date of the first anniversary of the conflict with Hungary. To mark this event, pilots (from left to right) slobodniks Jozef Drlicka and Martin Ziaran, desiatnik Martin Danihel and rotnik Frantisek Hanovec are awarded decorations by the commander-in-chief of the Slovak air force, Gen Anton Pulanich. Ziaran and Hanovec together shot down a Polish Lublin R-XIII on 6 September 1939, this being the sole kill credited to the Slovak fighter force during the invasion of Poland (*via S Androvic*)

In fact, no Fiat was officially credited either to Hanovec or Danihel, and the Hungarians said none of their aircraft had been lost in aerial combat. They did, however, admit the loss of the CR.32 of Sgt Arpad Kertesz. Although it had taken part in the fight, Hungarian sources insisted that it was shot down by 'friendly' anti-aircraft fire, and that the pilot had baled out. The Slovak fighters would have to wait almost six months to score their first confirmed kill.

Later that day, Slovak territory was bombed for the first time when Spisska Nova Ves airfield was attacked by ten Hungarian Junkers Ju 86K-2 bombers from the *bombazoszazad 3/4 Sarkany* and *3/5 Huvelyk Matyi*. Although 12 soldiers and civilians were killed, with 17 injured and six aircraft damaged in the raid, the Hungarians failed to knock the airfield out of operation. The only Slovak pilot who managed to take off was No 39 Sqn's catnik Frantisek Cyprich, but he was unable to catch the departing bombers in his B 534. A future ace with 14 confirmed kills and one unconfirmed destroyed, Cyprich would eventually get another chance to shoot down a Hungarian aircraft five years later during the Slovak National Uprising. This time, he would take full advantage of the opportunity.

On 26 March 1939 an armistice was signed, and two days later the fighting stopped as the diplomats took over from the soldiers. Two years later both Slovaks and Hungarians would join the attack on the Soviet Union.

THE POLISH EPISODE

On 1 September 1939, units of Hitler's *Wehrmacht*, supported by the Luftwaffe, rolled into Poland. They were also backed by the Slovak armed forces. The Slovak government had already given consent to a German

attack from its territory, but its ground units did not penetrate far into Poland. They limited themselves to regaining the regions of Orava, Spis and Javorina, which had been annexed by Poland in 1920, 1924 and in 1938, the latter in accordance with the Munich Agreement.

Participation by air force units comprised two squadrons, Nos 12 (at Spisska Nova Ves) and 15 (at Zvolen), each with ten S 328s to provide tactical reconnaissance ahead of the advancing land forces. Nos 45 and 49 Sqns (both at Spisska Nova Ves) were assigned to escort the Letovs with 20 B 534s. They also conducted several escort missions for the Ju 87B Stukas of III./StG 2 'Immelmann' on raids against Polish railway targets near Lvov and Drogobytch. The Slovaks lost two B 534s, both on 9 September. One crashed, killing desiatnik Viliam Jaloviar, while the other was shot down by Polish anti-aircraft fire, sending catnik Viliam Grun into captivity, from which he later managed to escape.

During the campaign, Slovakian fighters shot down just one Polish aircraft – the first confirmed kill officially credited to them. It happened on 6 September. A formation of three No 45 Sqn B 534s scrambled from Narsany advanced airstrip west of Sabinov, under the leadership of rotnik Frantisek Hanovec (the man whose Hungarian CR.32 kill of six months earlier had not been confirmed), to intercept a Polish reconnaissance aircraft. Flying as his wingmen were desiatniks Martin Ziaran and Viliam Jaloviar. Soon after take-off, they spotted a Lublin R-XIII two-seat reconnaissance aircraft of 56 *Eskadra*, operating from Mrowli, near Rzeszow. It had been tasked with performing a tactical reconnaissance mission over Bochnia, Nowy Sacz, Spisska Nova Ves, Presov and Bardejov.

This archaic aircraft was easy meat for the three Avias, and it was soon sent down in flames at Ostrovany, near Narsany. The pilot, Corp Edward Piasecki, and the observer, Lt Edward Porada, were both killed. The victory was shared equally by all three members of the Avia formation. It was also the first kill to be officially credited to Hanovec, who added five more on the eastern front as member of the 13(*slow*)./JG 52.

ON THE EASTERN FRONT

Only after the end of the Polish campaign was it possible to reorganise the Slovak Air Force. The reorganisation was conducted in several phases, and was not completed until the beginning of 1940. The original five fighter squadrons were merged to create three, which received the numbers 11 (stationed in Piestany), 12 (Spisska Nova Ves) and 13 (Piestany). From

B 534s of No 37 Sqn (the forerunner of No 13 Sqn) are seen on the ground between sorties during the Polish campaign of September 1939. They display the second version of the Slovakian national insignia, which was used from 10 September 1939 until 15 October 1940, together with the German *Balkenkreuzen*. The first insignia, applied from 23 June 1939, had no white outline

Zasavik Frantisek Hanovec was a veteran of all of Slovakia's war time campaigns. He fought the Hungarians and Poles in 1939, the Russians in the 1941, 1942 and 1943 campaigns, the Americans in 1944 and finally the Germans during the uprising. He scored six confirmed kills, including five Soviet aircraft (Airacobra, Boston, Yak-1, Il-2 and La-5) and one Polish machine. Two further claims – a Hungarian Fiat CR.32 and a German Ju 88 – remained unconfirmed. He shared in the first Slovak fighter kill when, on 6 September 1939, he shot down a Polish Lublin R-XIII reconnaissance machine near the village of Narsany

The Slovakian aviation industry was practically non-existent both before and during the war, so the repair of damaged aircraft and the replacement of those lost in combat was difficult to manage. However, the modest damage inflicted on B 534 No 158, seen here after it had been involved in an accident at Piestany on 22 January 1940, would have been repaired in the frontline. The aircraft was assigned to No 37 Sqn at the time. No 13 Sqn was formed out of this unit nine days after this photograph was taken

20 April 1940, all three were concentrated into the 2nd Fighter Wing (*stihaci perut II*), headquartered at Piestany. Each of the squadrons was equipped with B 534s and Bk 534s.

There would be only one further major organisational change in the Slovak fighter air force during the war when, on 1 June 1943, the 3rd Fighter Wing (*stihaci perut III*) was formed at Piestany. It incorporated

This Slovak Air Arms flying school B 534 at Trencianske Biskupice aerodrome displays the national insignia valid from 15 October 1940 until the Slovak National Uprising in 1944

Cannon-armed Bk 534 No 519 (M-8) was photographed on the eastern front in the summer of 1941. It was frequently flown by catnik Jan Reznak during this period of near constant base moves and combat. The letters K, L and M were used by Nos 11, 12 and 13 Sqns respectively (*J Reznak*)

Although the SVZ was short of equipment, its most acute deficiency was in personnel. New pilots were trained at the flying school (LS-SVZ) at Piestany (from April 1940), Trencianske Biskupice (from October 1940) and finally Tri Duby (from August 1943). Here, a group of nine future fighter pilots pose in front of a B 534 fighter-trainer at Trencianske Biskupice in 1941. They are, from left to right, Rudolf Bozik, Ernest Trebaticky, Jan Koval, Stefan Ocvirk, Jan Kalisky, Pavol Kalmancok, Robert Mitosinka, Karol Geletko and Frantisek Bosmansky. Bozik and Ocvirk would later become aces with twelve and five kills respectively (*via K Geletko*)

No 13 Sqn and the newly-formed No 14 Sqn. At that time the former, equipped with Bf 109Gs, was active on the eastern front, while the latter was flying old Bf 109Es bought in Germany, but had not yet been activated. Only Nos 11 and 12 Sqns remained in the 2nd Fighter Wing, both equipped with obsolete B 534s. The first was intended to be rearmed with Ju 87D-5 Stuka dive-bombers, but this did not happen. By then, the Slovaks had been fighting on the eastern front for two years.

Slovakian ground forces were comprised of the Army Corps (*Armadny sbor*) and the Rapid Group (*Rychla skupina,* soon to be renamed Rapid Brigade or *Rychla brigada*), while the Securing Division remained in the

Seen shortly before No 13 Sqn left for the eastern front, catnik Jan Reznak – then still an unknown young fighter pilot – sits in the cockpit of his B 534 at Piestany in June 1941. He was to become the top Slovakian ace with 32 confirmed kills (*J Reznak*)

His cockpit open, Jan Reznak closes up with his wingman in his B 534 during a patrol near Yarmolincy, in the Ukraine, in July 1941 (*J Reznak*)

rear. The Rapid Division was the Slovak Army's most modern and most mobile element, and it advanced via Lvov, Kiev and Rostov into the Caucasus.

Air support was provided by Slovak Air Arms units led by Gen Anton Pulanich, with podpluknovik Emil Novotny as his chief of staff. The vanguard was formed by the 1st Observation Wing (under Maj Kornel Jancek), with Nos 1, 2 and 3 Sqns having a total number of 30 S 328s. The 2nd Fighter Wing, under stotnik Vladimir Kacka, was comprised of Nos 11, 12 and 13 Sqns and their 33 B 534s, as well as a liaison unit.

In the days immediately after the declaration of war, these units were transferred from their peacetime bases to airfields in eastern Slovakia, and they did not begin their move in to western Ukraine until 7 July 1941. But as this left Slovakia virtually without air defence, No 11 Sqn soon returned to Piestany.

During their first combat deployment to the eastern front, the Slovak squadrons were on the move continuously through Galicia and the Ukraine, flying from one field after another in rapid succession. Opposition from the Red Air Force over what became known as the Stalin Line was pitiful as most of its aircraft had been destroyed by surprise attacks on its airfields in the first hours of the campaign. Anti-aircraft fire was a more dangerous enemy, however, and caused the loss of several aircraft.

In fact, it was this anti-aircraft fire that was to lead to the first feat of conspicuous bravery in the short history of the Slovak Air Arms. On the morning of 25 July 1941, while escorting a Henschel Hs 126 reconnaissance machine, a three-aircraft section of B 534s of No 13 Sqn ran into heavy flak . The fighter of catnik Frantisek Brezina (a future ace with 14 kills to his credit) was badly damaged, and the pilot made an emergency landing deep inside Red Army territory near the village of Trojstjancy.

While the Soviets directed a hail of fire against Brezina's aircraft, fellow pilot catnik Stefan Martis (later to be credited with five kills) made several strafing attacks on the Red Army soldiers and then landed to save his comrade. Brezina jumped onto the lower left wing of his rescuer's machine and clutched a strut while Martis immediately opened the throttle of his fighter. Although the Soviets opened fire and slightly wounded Martis in the leg, he managed to take off. However, moments

B 534s of No 12 Sqn are dispersed among wrecked SB-2bis and SB-3 bombers abandoned by the retreating Soviets at an airfield in the Ukraine in the summer of 1941. The squadron was the only SVZ unit to score aerial kills during the 1941 campaign when, on 7 and 8 September 1941, its pilots claimed three I-16 fighters (*via A Droppa*)

A three-aircraft section of Slovak B 534s overfly the flat and featureless steppe during an escort mission in the Ukraine in the summer of 1941

During the Russian campaign, No 13 Sqn's catnik Stefan Martis returned to base on 25 July 1941 with a passenger – catnik Frantisek Brezina – who was standing on the wing clutching a strut. Brezina had been shot down over Russian territory and Martis landed to save him from being captured. Both these photographs were taken at Piestany, in Slovakia, during a filmed reconstruction of this dramatic event the following October. Simulating Martis' aircraft is a No 11 Sqn B 534 (as indicated by the fuselage letter K), but Brezina's part in the reconstruction was 'played' by a dummy. Both men later became aces with 13(slow)./JG 52

For his heroism in rescuing the downed Frantisek Brezina on 25 July 1941, Stefan Martis was awarded the Slovak Silver Medal for Heroism and the German Eisernkreuz II. Klasse. Flying with 13(slow)./JG 52, he later claimed the destruction of five Soviet aircraft (three Il-2s and two Yak-1s), but in July 1944 he was released from active service due to illness. Martis flew as a commercial pilot between 1949 and 1953, and later worked as a car resprayer and excavator driver (via M Fekets)

after becoming airborne Brezina's legs slid off the wing, leaving him precariously hanging onto the strut. He could easily have fallen, and since Martis had to fly at full throttle, Brezina, his strength beginning to fail, had to wait for him to slow down before he could pull himself back up onto the wing. Eventually, B 534 No 181, its tank punctured, landed safely back at Tulczyn airfield.

This episode was repeated just five days later when No 12 Sqn attacked ground targets on the Uman-Novoarchangelsk road. B 534 No 242, piloted by catnik Martin Danihel (a veteran of combat with Hungarian fighters), was forced down in no man's land near the village of Babanka. He was rescued by catnik Jozef Drlicka, and they landed safely at their Gajsin base.

The first clash between Slovak and Soviet fighters came on 29 July, and ended without loss to either side. But within a few weeks there were more frequent combats on the approaches to Kiev, and No 12 Sqn shot down three Polikarpov I-16s. On 7 September, at 1850 hrs, ten B 534s scrambled from Gubin airfield to intercept nine I-16s. Catnik Jozef Drlicka shot down one which hit the ground near Gornostajpol, 44 miles (70 km) north of Kiev. The Russian pilot did not bale out. According to German flak battery reports, another I-16 had been shot down during the same combat, but this was not claimed by the Slovaks. It may have been accounted for by the other two members of Drlicka's formation, rotnik Frantisek Hanovec or catnik Martin Danihel.

The next day, while patrolling over the Dniepr bridge, three B 534s encountered two I-16s, one of which was shot down into Borki forest, east of Ostyerkby, by catnik Ivan Kocka. It was the third, and final, Soviet aircraft credited to Slovak airmen in 1941, for although they engaged in several more dogfights with the enemy, they did not manage to increase their score.

The decreasing number of combat-worthy aircraft, their deteriorating condition and a shortage of spares and fuel resulted in the SVZ units gradually withdrawing to Slovakia. On 15 August No 13 Sqn returned to Piestany, followed by No 12 Sqn on 29 October, and both units were virtually back to peacetime service in their own country – but not for long. By the following summer Slovak units were back on the eastern front, where combat was renewed in earnest.

On 22 June 1942 No 1 Observation Squadron left Slovakia with six S 328s, followed eight days later by No 11 Sqn with its 12 B 534s. But obsolete equipment relegated these units to operations against partisans behind the frontline in the Zhitomir, Ovruc and Minsk areas. Reconnaissance flights, ground attack and bombing missions were carried out until 25 October 1943, when No 11 Sqn returned home once more, but this time for re-equipment.

Frantisek Brezina was a veteran of the eastern front and of the anti-German uprising. He claimed 14 kills and served with the Czechoslovak Air Force as an instructor post-war. He was badly injured on 1 July 1949 when his Siebel Si 204E crashed near Caslav. Subsequently grounded, Brezina left the service in 1952 with the rank of lieutenant

No 13 Sqn pilots enjoy the war summer sun alongside a B 534 while being held at readiness in mid-1941. Dark patches on the fighter's lower wing reveal where battle damage has recently been repaired

A cannon-armed Bk 534 fitted with Slovak-made skis has its engine run-up at Trencianske Biskupice aerodrome. Skis were used in field conditions only during 1942, when No 11 Sqn fought Soviet partisans in the Ukraine and Byelorussia

EASTERN FRONT

O n 26 February 1942, 105 Slovakian airmen led by Maj Vladimir Kacka left their homeland for a long train journey. The party, which included 19 fighter pilots, was bound for Karup-Grøve airfield in occupied Denmark. There, German instructors were to teach them how to fly and service Messerschmitt Bf 109E fighters in a unit that was designated 5(*Slowakei*). *Schul-Staffel Jagdgruppe* Drontheim.

The theory section of the training course started on 3 March, and was followed by practical flying training starting on the 27th. The Slovak pilots received basic training in Arado Ar 96B training aircraft before moving on to the Bf 109B and D and finally the *Emil*. All the students were experienced pilots, so their training progressed relatively smoothly. The training culminated with firing at ground targets between 15 and 18 June, and officially ended on 1 July.

If training Slovak fighter pilots to fly the Bf 109 was relatively straightforward, the same could not be said for the acquisition of the new equipment. Instead of the 12 Bf 109E-7s that had been offered, two E-2s, one E-3, five E-4s and four E-7s were eventually ferried home by Slovak pilots between 1 July and 5 September. The aircraft were well-worn examples which had seen combat in France, over Britain and in North Africa. Some had been crashed and repaired several times. In any case, by that time the *Emil* had been replaced in frontline Luftwaffe service by the more modern Bf 109F. For now, though, they represented the most up-to-date equipment available to the Slovak Air Force.

Combat-weary Bf 109Es used by the Luftwaffe in Western Europe and North Africa were the first modern fighters issued to the SVZ. The Slovaks received more than 20 worn-out *Emils* from the Germans in 1942-43 (*via J Janecka*)

Bf 109E-4 Wk-Nr 2028 still wore German national insignia and the manufacturer's radio codes (D-I+W??) when photographed soon after its delivery to Slovakia in 1942. Along with two dozen other *Emils*, this aircraft was ferried east from Wiener Neustadt via Aspern, where it was damaged on 13 August 1942 during a force landing by stotnik Ondrej Dumbala (No 13 Sqn CO). It is seen at Trencianske Biskupice, where SVZ machines were repaired (*via S Androvic*)

Of the 19 pilots retrained in Denmark, 14 were assigned to No 13 Sqn at Piestany, where they formed what was called the first front team, soon to be deployed to the eastern front. The pilots were stotnik Ondrej Dumbala (CO), poruciks Vladimir Krisko (deputy CO) and Jan Gerthofer, rotniks Frantisek Cyprich and Jozef Drlicka and catniks Frantisek Brezina, Jozef Jancovic, Stefan Martis, Jan Reznak, Jan Setvak, Jozef Stauder, Jozef Svejdik, Jozef Vincur and Pavol Zelenak. Their average age was no more than 25.

Preparation for combat involved special flying training at Piestany and target practice at the Malacky-Novy Dvor firing range in western Slovakia. The final firing exercises on 25 September were witnessed by the Chief of Staff podpluknovnik Alojz Ballay and the Chief of the

A Slovak Bf 109E flies over the Povazi Valle during a training sortie soon after its arrival in Slovakia. Most of the *Emils* were used by No 13 Sqn on the Eastern Front, while others, like this example, served as training aircraft until 1944 (*via J Janecka*)

The same trio of No 13 Sqn Bf 109Es seen on page 20 close up for a spot of formation flying practice prior to their departure with the first front team to the eastern front (*via J Janecka*)

The official leave-taking ceremony for the flying element of the first front team took place in the presence of the SVZ Chief of Staff, podplukovnik Alojz Ballay, at Piestany in October 1942. The five pilots visible in this line up are, from left to right, stotnik Ondrej Dumbala (No 13 Sqn CO), porucik Jan Gerthofer, rotniks Frantisek Cyprich and Jozef Drlicka and catnik Jozef Svejdik. The latter two pilots were subsequently killed in combat over the Caucasus

Deutsche Luftwaffenmission in der Slovakei, Generalmajor Ludwig Keiper. Both senior officers professed themselves satisfied and No 13 Sqn was duly declared fully combat-worthy, and thus ready for deployment to the eastern front.

On 14 October the groundcrew (plus five pilots for whom no *Emils* were available) left Piestany for their new base of Maikop, at the foot of the Caucasus, some 44 miles (70 km) south-east of Krasnodar. There, they were to prepare for aircraft which arrived between 27 October and 4 November. Like its Croat predecessor, 15(*Kroat*)./JG 52, the Slovak squadron was assigned for tactical operational purposes to a Luftwaffe unit, in this instance II./JG 52, and it appears in German records as 13(*slow*)./JG 52.

Stotnik (later major) Ondrej Dumbala (left), long-time No 13 Sqn CO, led the first front team until April 1943. He scored just one victory (an I-16 on 18 January 1943 near Smolenskaya) in that time. Here, he talks to nadporucik Jan Gerthofer, who claimed 26 confirmed kills to become the third ranking Slovakian ace

The Slovak fighters made their first flights from the new base on 9 November and their first encounter with the Soviet Air Force is recorded as having taken place on the 29th. During a *freie jagd* mission between 0830 and 0930 hrs in the vicinity of Tuapse, a two-aircraft section comprising porucik Vladimir Krisko and catnik Jozef Jancovic engaged a numerically superior force of nine Soviet Polikarpov I-153 biplanes, mistakenly referred to in German records as 'Curtiss' fighters. On their return, the Slovak pilots reported that three Soviet aeroplanes had been shot down, although these kills were not officially confirmed by the German RLM. It was therefore catnik Frantisek Brezina who achieved the first officially-confirmed Slovak victory on 12 December when he shot down a MiG-3 fighter over Tuapse at 1347 hrs.

Bf 109E-4 Wk-Nr 3317 'White 7' served with No 13 Sqn's first front team, being transferred to the eastern front in October 1942. Here, catnik Stefan Martis (a future ace with five kills) poses in front the aircraft, which survived many combat sorties and several crash-landings to return to Slovakia. On 12 April 1944 14-kill ace *zastavnik* Frantisek Brezina belly-landed the aircraft for a final time near Vajnory. Although he emerged from the wreckage without injury, Wk-Nr 3317 was written off

German national insignia on Slovak *Emils* was progressively over-sprayed. Bf 109E-4 Wk-Nr 2945 displays Slovak crosses on the fuselage and wings, but the swastika is still worn on the tail. It is also evident from this photograph that some experimentation was undertaken with tactical numbers on the fuselage, as this aircraft carries the same numerals twice, but in different sizes

Later, the aircraft retained only the smaller number behind the fuselage cross, although, as in this case, traces of the larger number – and the swastika on the tail – remain. The propeller spinner is yellow. This photograph was taken in October 1942, shortly before the No 13 Sqn first front team moved to the eastern front. 'White 2' was occasionally flown over the Caucasus by future aces catnik Jan Reznak and rotnik Pavel Zelenak. After the squadron received *Friedrichs* and later *Gustavs*, this *Emil* was repaired and flown back to Slovakia to serve as a training aircraft for other future aces, including rotnik Stefan Martis and catnik Rudolf Bozik. Later still, it was assigned to a readiness force, which was duly increased to squadron strength. The veteran fighter was then flown by aces zastavnik Frantisek Brezina, Jozef Stauder and Pavel Zelenak once again (*via J Sehnal*)

In the following weeks No 13 Sqn's operational activity consisted mostly of free hunting sorties, escort missions for German bombers, ground-attack and transport and reconnaissance aircraft and airfield defence. But right from the start of the deployment, the unit suffered from a shortage of aircraft, and by the end of November it could field only three combat-worthy Bf 109Es out of the eight with which it had started six weeks earlier.

In the wake of an agreement between the German DLM and RLM and the Slovak Ministry of National Defence (*Ministerstvo narodnej obrany*, MNO), it was decided to re-equip No 13 Sqn with Bf 109F-4s. The first was received on 18 December 1942, and because training on the new equipment had to be done in parallel with the squadron's operational duties, 13(*slow*)./JG 52 flew a mix of both types for a time. As the aircraft were of German origin, they not only wore standard Luftwaffe camouflage but also carried German national insignia. Later, their pilots' nationality would be indicated by the red, blue and white Slovak colours displayed on the propeller spinners of their fighters.

The unit remained at Maikop until 3 January 1943, when it moved to an airfield at Krasnodar, in Kuban. There, its score began to mount. On 17 January future ranking Slovakian ace catnik Jan Reznak scored his first kill. It was the squadron's seventh, and for Reznak it came as the climax to a day of drama. He later recalled;

Above and left
Some of the Bf 109Es displayed the insignia of the No 13 Sqn first front team on their engine cowlings prior to their transfer to the eastern front. The colours of the emblem are thought to be a white cross, blue hills and a red sun (*via S Androvic*)

'I took off at 0620 hrs from Krasnodar in my Bf 109F-2 (Wk-Nr 12004) as wingman to nadporucik Krisko (a future ace with nine kills). We were to escort a German Fw 189 reconnaissance aircraft which was supposed to photograph Russian positions at Kuban from an altitude of 2000 m (6500 ft). It was nice sunny weather and visibility was excellent. Small clouds from exploding Russian anti-aircraft shells made us aware that we had just crossed the frontline. At that moment I spotted dots moving on the horizon. I called on the radio, "Attention. Indians ahead!" It was a formation of four I-153 fighters. One immediately detached from the formation and headed directly for the Fw 189. Krisko took care of him. I attacked the remaining three Russians.

'They were flying in a line, and tried to get behind me in a wide curve. At that moment, when the first was getting into a firing position, I started to climb steeply. I escaped from him and attacked the last Russian aircraft in the line. The pilot realised my intention and used his skill to escape.

'After he escaped – at that time I didn't have much experience – I chased the other two. In a steep climb, I got behind the last one. Then things happened fast. Immediately I got him in my sights, I fired a short burst which hit the *Chaika's* fuselage. It dived and exploded in a cloud of dark smoke after hitting the snow-covered ground west of Smolenskaya.

'The remaining three *Chaikas* started to escape but I pursued them. They were below me and I quickly caught them, but another six then attacked me from above. I broke away into the sun and escaped. Then I saw that all nine Russians had joined into one group and were circling over one spot. This was my chance. I immediately attacked with the sun at my back, and after my second pass a *Chaika* dived away, trailing smoke. But I had fallen into a trap. Suddenly, one of the Russians fired a flare. The *Chaikas* parted in all directions and anti-aircraft shells started to explode around my aircraft. I realised that the Russians had wanted to lure me over their anti-aircraft artillery. But the trap didn't work because I managed to dodge the flak and escape.

'During the return flight I spotted four Petlyakov Pe-2 bombers heading for Krasnodar. They were flying in a line and I targeted the second aircraft from the right and attacked it from behind. I was quite close and I got into his slipstream. I probably didn't hit him because he continued flying. The Russian gunners in all four aircraft then woke up and I found myself the target for their heavy fire. I broke off to make another attack, but the Russians didn't wait. Hastily, they dropped their bombs on the fields below and escaped at high speed. I landed at Krasnodar at 0724 hrs. Five minutes later the Fw 189 returned, escorted by Krisko.'

It is possible that Reznak's first victim came from 975 IAP. Records show that an I-153 flown by Capt Filatov failed to return from a sortie near Novodmitriyevskaya – only three miles from Smolenskaya, where Reznak claimed his success.

A few hours later, at 1331 hrs, Reznak took off for another combat mission, this time in Bf 109E-4 (Wk-Nr 2787), but his luck seemed to have deserted him. He flew with Gerthofer, Cyprich and Brezina on a *Freie Jagd*;

'Four LaGG-3 fighters were flying at approximately 2000 m (6500 ft) over Krasnodar. I was the first to spot them. I called, "Attention. Four Indians ahead of us". They tried to hide in the glare of the sun. I was slightly behind the others, so the Russians probably took me for easy meat. And what's more, I found that my guns wouldn't fire. But the first LaGG-3 was already coming at me. One of his undercarriage legs was not properly retracted, but the Russian obviously didn't care because he started firing like a madman. When I looked behind I saw two more shooting at me. Fortunately for me the Russians, greedy for the kill, were interfering with each other in this chaos.

'Nevertheless, I was hit. Suddenly, I felt an impact and a jerk. My *Emil* was spinning down and I was only able to pull out at the last moment. Punched in my left wing were three big holes from Russian 20 mm ShVAK cannon. I barely managed to limp home over the rooftops.

'Flying just above the ground, I was too low to bale out. I was very lucky to land at Krasnodar at 1408 hrs. The groundcrew counted 60 holes caused by 7.62 mm machine gun rounds, while one of the three cannon hits broke the left wing spar. It was a wonder that I made it home with such a wreck. After I landed I was told that "Jano" Gerthofer had got one of those rascals.'

Gerthofer's victim was possibly LaGG-3 No 2666 'White 25', flown by Sgt Oleg I Gavrilov of 269 IAP. Reznak's third sortie of the day, another *Freie Jagd* mission in the Novorossiysk-Krymskaya area with Gerthofer and Cyprich in Bf 109F-4 Wk-Nr 13334, was uneventful.

Soviet pressure on the German 17th Army in the Taman Peninsula hastened the transfer of 13(*slow*)./JG 52 to other bases. The evacuation of Krasnodar started on 31 January when the first elements of the squadron fled to Slavyanskaya airfield. But the Soviet offensive continued, and the unit retreated to Kerch IV, in the Crimea, on 16 and 17 February. By this time No 13 Sqn had 21 confirmed victories to its credit. Brezina with four was the top scorer, followed by Reznak and Jancovic both with three.

The squadron's growing successes caught German attention, and 13(*slow*)./JG 52 was again re-equipped shortly afterwards. The remaining six *Friedrichs* had all been returned by 5 March to be replaced by nine brand-new Bf 109G-2s. By the end of the same month, however, they had been exchanged for G-4s with more effective FuG 16Z radio sets which had greater range and were easier to operate than the previous FuG VIIa. Many aircraft were modified into Bf 109G-4/R6s through the fitment of two extra underwing MG 151 20 mm cannon, whilst some became Bf 109G-4/Trops with dust filters. The arrival of the *Gustavs* brought the Slovak squadron up to the same standard of equipment as the rest of *Jagdgeschwader* 52.

The re-equipment process was, however, completed only after yet another change of base. On 17 and 18 March the squadron moved across the Kerch Channel to Taman airfield on the peninsula of the same name. Here, the unit became embroiled in a series of intense actions that saw No 13 Sqn's victory tally rapidly increase. The unit remained at Taman until 1 April when it moved again, this time to Anapa airfield on the Black Sea coast, where the Slovak fighters were to remain for some time.

This rare photograph, taken at Krasnodar on 20 January 1943, shows catnik Jozef Jancovic pointing out the severe combat damage inflicted on his Bf 109F. He had just returned from a mission with a piece of I-16 wing embedded in his aircraft as a result of a head-on encounter which had ended with the Soviet pilot trying to ram him

A 'black man' busily services the engine of a Slovakian Bf 109G-4/R6 bearing fuselage tactical number 'Yellow 11', as well as traces of its German radio codes

Growing combat experience, and the latest equipment, were the two factors that brought further successes, and the Slovak pilots' scores continued to rise. From only three kills in December 1942, the monthly totals grew to 12 for January 1943, eight in February and no fewer than 44 in March 1943, when operational activity reached a peak.

But these successes were achieved at a price, for four Slovak fighter pilots were killed. On the morning of 2 January rotnik Jozef Drlicka failed to return from combat with a larger group of Soviet LaGG-3s east of Tuapse, in the Caucasus. On the 17th catnik Jozef Vincur was shot down (apparently in error by German flak) during combat with a mixed group of I-16 and I-153s, his machine diving at full speed into the ground near the village of Smolenskaya, south-east of Krasnodar.

Two weeks later, on the 31st, rotnik Jozef Svejdik failed to return from a *Freie Jagd* sortie near Kropotkin airfield. He was probably shot down by Soviet anti-aircraft fire. The fourth loss was a particularly grievous blow because the victim was seven-victory ace rotnik Jozef Jancovic. On 29 March he took off from Taman as wingman to rotnik Frantisek Cyprich to intercept Soviet Il-2 *Stormoviks* ground-attack machines that were raiding Taman docks.

'Jozo' Jancovic was one of the squadron's most aggressive pilots. 'He was', said Jan Reznak, 'like a bird of prey who never took any account of his own safety in air combat'. The most successful Slovak fighter pilot added, 'One of the things I liked about him was the way he was not afraid of dogfights'.

On that fateful day Jancovic's aggressive nature proved to be his undoing. Both Slovak pilots pursued the fleeing Il-2s over the Sea of Azov but then escorting LaGG-3s joined the combat. Jancovic, chasing the last *Stormovik*, made the fatal mistake of concentrating exclusively on his target. He was catching the Il-2, and was just about to open fire, when his Bf 109G-2 (Wk-Nr 14380) shuddered after being hit by Soviet fire. Jancovic was wounded in the left leg, and he attempted an emergency belly landing on uneven terrain near the village of Akhtanizovskaya.

The aircraft was completely written-off in the subsequent crash and Jancovic suffered further serious injuries when he hit his head on the gunsight as the aircraft lurched to a standstill. Rumanian soldiers took him to the field medical station in the village of Zaporozhskaya, about 20 miles (30 km) east of Kerch, where German doctors gave him first aid. Jancovic was too badly injured, however, and he died the following morning. He was the only Slovak ace to die on the eastern front.

Nadporucnik Jan Gerthofer (26 kills) is greeted by rotnik Izidor Kovarik upon his return from a successful sortie in 'Yellow 10'. With 28 confirmed kills, 'Izo' Kovarik had become the second ranking Slovak ace by the time he was killed in the crash of his Gotha Go 145 trainer biplane near Tri Duby airfield on 11 July 1944

Catnik Jozef Jancovic was an aggressive Slovak pilot who never shirked the hardest sorties and never avoided combat, whatever the odds. After scoring seven confirmed kills, he was fatally wounded in Bf 109G-2 Wk-Nr 14380 when he was bounced by a LaGG-3 over the Sea of Azov on 29 March 1943. Jancovic crash-landed near the village of Akhtanizovskaya and died the next day in a field hospital in Zaporoshskaya. He was the fourth, and last, fighter pilot of 13(*slow*)./JG 52 to die in combat over the Caucasus and Kuban (*via M Krajci*)

Factory-fresh 13(*slow*)./JG 52 Bf 109G-4/R6 had only just been delivered to the unit when this photograph was taken, the fighter still bearing its factory codes CU+PQ on the fuselage and wing undersurfaces. These would be quickly oversprayed once in the frontline This shot was taken as the machine was being ferried from Kerch to Anapa on 16 April 1943. It was occasionally flown by rotnik Frantisek Brezlna (14 kills) (*via S Androvic*)

The Slovakian *Emils* had led hard lives in Luftwaffe service prior to them being issued to No 13 Sqn, and the years of wear and tear caused frequent engine and undercarriage failures, much to the alarm of the squadron pilots. This machine was belly-landed by catnik Stefan Jambor following engine failure in 1943. The pilot was unhurt

During the March battles 13(*slow*)/JG 52 achieved its 50th confirmed victory – claimed by porucik Jan Gerthofer. At 1128 hrs on the 21st he shot down a Petlyakov Pe-2 reconnaissance aircraft over the Black Sea south of Myschako. It was the first of the type to fall to the squadron, and the feat generated numerous messages of congratulation, including one from the Luftwaffe's Commander-in-Chief, Reichsmarshall Hermann Göring himself.

Several months of intensive deployment not only cost lives but also placed intense strain on the surviving pilots. It was quite clear that they needed relief, and CO, Maj Ondrej Dumbala, requested a change of personnel. Slovak HQ responded promptly by running a training course for 13 hand-picked pilots on the Bf 109E. Once this had been completed, the pilots concerned formed what was known as the second front team, destined to relieve their predecessors. Stotnik Jozef Palenicek was appointed CO, but he had only been in the job a few days when he was made CO of No 13 Sqn's first front team. He assumed command on the 20th. Maj Dumbala, who had been taken ill in the field, headed back to Slovakia and went on to run the training of reserve pilots on Bf 109s.

Palenicek assumed command of 13(*slow*)./JG 52 at a time when the struggle for air supremacy over Kuban (17 April to 7 June 1943) was just beginning. In this battle, Slovak fighter pilots became involved in their most intense air encounters yet with numerically superior Soviet forces.

'In the sector to which the squadron has been assigned, enemy air activity has increased to such an extent that pilots – mainly on escort flights – have to engage with forces up to nine times more numerous', Palenicek reported back to Slovakia. 'In our sector English Spitfires and, before that, American Airacobras have now appeared'. These were aircraft which Palenicek thought had features that 'equalled both the Messerschmitt Bf 109G-2 and G-4.'

A pair of Slovakian Bf 109G-4/R6s prepare to taxi out at the start of yet another sortie from Anapa in April 1943. 'Yellow 1' was occasionally flown by rotnik Izidor Kovarik (28 kills) and nadporucik Vladimir Krisko (nine kills). After re-equipment with *Gustavs*, the pilots of 13(*slow*)./JG 52 were soon able to demonstrate total mastery of their new mounts. The arrival of these machines coincided with an increase in aerial combat, and the Slovakian pilots' overall tally rose rapidly. The 50th kill was gained on 21 March, the 100th on 27 April, the 150th on 20 June and the 200th on 24 September 1943 (*via J Sehnal*)

With the intensity of fighting over Kuban, it did not take long for 13(*slow*)./JG 52's score to climb to the magic 100 mark. The 100th victory came on 27 April, and was achieved by Jan Reznak who, at 1748 hrs, shot down a LaGG-3 near Kholmskaya station. In this situation multiple victories were not exceptional, with two pilots managing to destroy as many as four aircraft each in a single day.

For example, on 24 April porucik Jan Gerthofer shot down two LaGG-3s, an Il-2 *Stormovik* and a Boston bomber. Rotnik Izidor Kovarik

Inseparable friends, and the unit's most successful pilots, rotniks Jan Reznak (left) and Izidor Kovarik pose with Bf 109G-4 'Yellow 10' at Anapa in late April 1943

'Black men' of 13(*slow*)./JG 52 uncrate spare parts in the spring of 1943. Note the German Bf 109G-4 parked behind them

matched this feat on 29 May by downing four Yak-1 fighters. Both pilots claimed their kills during the course of two separate sorties flown on these dates.

Despite the mounting score, the unit's own losses remained modest, and were caused by bombing rather than air combat. Indeed, after Jozef Jancovic's death, no other pilots from the squadron's first front team were killed or wounded. This was an exceptional statistic, considering that these pilots were not relieved by the second front team for a further three months.

This did not mean, however, that the pilots enjoyed good health. Physical and psychological exhaustion – the consequence of intense operational activity – began to take their toll. The first front team remained at Anapa, on the Black Sea coast, until its replacement by the second front team. The final kill claimed by the original pilots came on 4 July 1943, when at 1008 hrs nadporucik Vladimir Krisko shot down a Pe-2. The Soviet bomber fell near the small town of Akhtanizovskaya, and was Krisko's ninth, and last, kill. Three days later the first front team left for the ten-day train journey back to Slovakia.

The results of the squadron's eight-month combat deployment were impressive – 1504 combat sorties, 206 engagements with the enemy and 154 confirmed victories, with a further 16 unconfirmed. These successes had cost the squadron just four pilots dead or missing.

Jan Reznak, ace and cover star. The June 1943 issue of a Slovak language version of a magazine published by *Luftflotte 4* (*Luftflotte Südost* or *Vzdusna flota Juhovychod* in Slovak) featured a picture of the 13(*slow*)./JG 52 ace in the cockpit of a *Gustav* on its front cover. Here, Reznak reads the article about himself

A 'black man' of 13(*slow*)./JG 52 works on the engine of one of the unit's Bf 109G-4s at Anapa in April 1943. These aircraft were not Slovak property, which meant that they still displayed German national insignia. However, the operator's nationality was clearly indicated by the Slovak national colours of white, blue and red painted on the propeller spinner (*via M Krajci*)

Slovak aces pose together at Anapa in April 1943. They are, from left to right, rotnik Frantisek Cyprich (12 kills), Hauptmann Karl Thiem (Luftwaffe liaison officer) and rotniks Jan Reznak (32 kills), Izidor Kovarik (28 kills), Jozef Stauder (12 kills), Robert Nerad (chief-mechanic) and Pavol Zelenak (12 kills) (*via B Barbas*)

13(*slow*)./JG 52 Bf 109G-4 Wk-Nr 19347 'Yellow 9' taxies out for take-off at Anapa in late April 1943. Slovakian top scorer zastavnik Jan Reznak completed 20 combat sorties in this aircraft, scoring seven of his 32 confirmed kills with it. But as no pilot had any personal machine, it was flown by other pilots, including aces such as rotnik Frantisek Brezina, nadporucnik Vladimir Krisko and rotnik Stefan Martis. It fell into Russian hands when ace rotnik Anton Matusek defected on 9 September 1943 (*BA*)

The second front team, comprising nadporucik Juraj Puskar, rotniks Frantisek Hanovec, Frantisek Melichac, Stefan Jambor, Anton Matusek, Gustav Kubovic and Gustav Lang and catniks Ludovit Dobrovodsky, Alexander Geric, Rudolf Palaticky, Stefan Ocvirk, Karol Geletko and Rudolf Bozik, finally reached Piestany on 23 June 1943. The team was later joined by rotnik Stefan Martis, who had dropped out of the first team through illness in February. Most were young pilots (their

13(*slow*)./JG 52's medical officer, Aspirant MUDr Dubay, reads the issue of *Vzdusna flota Juhovychod* magazine that displayed Jan Reznak's picture on the cover at Anapa in June 1943. Behind him, Bf 109G-4 'Yellow 8' waits at readiness

Rotnik Sgt Jan Reznak, nadporucik Jan Gerthofer and Luftwaffe liaison officer Hauptmann Karl Thiem are engrossed in conversation alongside Bf 109G-4/Trop 'Yellow 10', whose fuselage shows traces of the original German radio codes having been crudely over-sprayed

Two Bf 109G-4s of 13(*slow*)./JG 52 sit at readiness at Anapa in the summer of 1943. 'Yellow 8' is the fighter furthest from the camera

Nadporucnik Vladimir Krisko was one of only three Slovakian officers to become an ace. As deputy CO of 13*(slow)*./JG 52, he claimed the destruction of nine Soviet aircraft, including four Yak-1s, two LaGG-3s and a single La-5, Il-2 and Pe-2. He commanded a readiness squadron on home defence duties and, during the uprising, a combined squadron. After the war Krisko led the 1st Air Regiment, and he left the Czechoslovak Air Force in 1951 with the rank of major

average age was just 24), who had accumulated minimal frontline flying experience back in Slovakia.

Their destination was not Anapa, which had been the first team's final base, but Sarabuz, in Crimea, for a short training course on the Bf 109G to enable them fly the *Gustav*. The unit was transported to Anapa by Ju 52/3m on 2 July. After a welcome by the CO, stotnik Jozef Palenicek, the unit began familiarisation flights before venturing into the combat

Rotnik Frantisek Hanovec of 13(*slow*)./JG 52 celebrates the second front team's first kill at Anapa on 22 July 1943 after downing a Soviet P-39 over Krymskaya. Hanovec opened his score in 1939 when he shared in the destruction of a Polish aircraft, and later shot down five Soviet machines in 1943. Helping him celebrate are, from left to right, unit deputy CO nadporucnik Juraj Puskar (five kills), rotnik Anton Matusek (12 kills), catnik Gustav Lang (two kills), rotnik Karol Duben (chief armourer), catnik Augustin Kubovic (one kill) and catnik Rudolf Palaticky (six kills)

Members of 13(slow)./JG 52 relax at Anapa, on the Black Sea coast, in the summer of 1943. Standing, from left to right, are rotnik Frantisek Hanovec (five confirmed kills plus one unconfirmed), catniks Augustin Kubovic (one kill) and Alexander Geric (nine kills), rotnik Anton Matusek (12 kills), nadporucnik Juraj Puskar (five kills) and catniks Frantisek Melichac (one kill) and Soska (mechanic). Seated, from left to right, are rotnik Stefan Martis (five kills) and catniks Ludovit Dobrovodsky (one kill) and Rudolf Palaticky (six kills)

Another Anapa photograph taken in the summer of 1943, showing, from left to right:, catnik Augustin Kubovic (one kill), rotnik Frantisek Hanovec (six kills), catniks Rudolf Bozik (eight) and Alexander Geric (nine kills), rotnik Anton Matusek (12 kills), stotnik Jozef Palenicek (13(slow)./JG 52 CO), Hauptmann Thiem (German liaison officer) and Hauptmann Helmut Kühle (*Gruppenkommandeur* of II./JG 52) (*via M Krajci*)

zone. However, prior to flying their first sorties, they were warned by the more experienced pilots to avoid being over-eager to score victories if they wanted to survive.

First success for the newcomers came on 22 July, and it was claimed by rotnik Frantisek Hanovec flying as wingman to nadporucik Juraj Puskar. At about 1145 hrs, they encountered four Airacobras, of which one was

The pilots seated in front of the 13(slow)./JG 52 Bf 109G-4s at Anapa in 1943 are, front row, from left to right, catnik Karol Geletko (one kill), rotnlk Frantlsek Hanovec (six kills) and catnik Stefan Martis (five kills) In the back row, from left to right, are rotnik Anton Matusek (12 kills), catnik Stefan Jambor, unknown, and German liaison officer Hauptmann Karl Thiem (*via B Barbas*)

SVZ veteran rotnik Stefan Jambor converses with his 'black men' from the cockpit of Bf 109G-4 'Yellow 1' – note the name *Marta* worn beneath the cockpit – at Anapa in the summer of 1943. Jambor was one of three Slovak pilots to be killed on 26 June 1944 in combat with the USAAF over southern Slovakia. His Bf 109G-6 'White 4' (Wk-Nr 161723) was riddled by machine gun fire from escorting Mustang fighters and it crashed between the villages of Hubice and Stvrtok na Ostrove (*K Geletko*)

Catnik Gustav Lang receives congratulations from Catnik Stefan Ocvirk after a successful sortie. This aircraft is *Marta*, seen above. Ocvirk claimed five kills on the eastern front (two Bostons, two LaGG-3s and a Yak-1), while Lang shot down an Il-2 and a LaGG-3. Lang's third success came on 26 June 1944 when he downed a B-24 Liberator flown by 2Lt Lincoln E Artz. He therefore became the only Slovakian fighter pilot to shoot down a US aircraft, but he paid for this success with his own life, for he was shot down by escorting P-38 Lightnings just moments later. Lang's Bf 109G-6 'White 10' (Wk-Nr 161713) crashed at Miloslavov na Ostrove, in southern Slovakia. He was found still strapped into the cockpit of the wrecked fighter, having made no attempt to bale out (*via J Rajninec*)

shot down by Hanovec after a hard fight. It crashed north of Krymskaya, but not before the pilot had safely baled out. More kills followed on the 26th when, between 1055 and 1130 hrs, catnik Rudolf Bozik downed an Airacobra and a Polikarpov R-5 reconnaissance machine. Another Airacobra and a Boston bomber were destroyed by rotnik Anton Matusek.

As operational activity intensified so the unit's victory tally increased. Although the second front team achieved only 11 kills in July, the Slovak pilots accounted for 21 Soviet aircraft in August and a further 16 in September. Most of these kills consisted of Lend-Lease Bostons, Airacobras and Spitfires – the first Spitfire fell to catnik Alexander Geric on 7 August.

The Slovak squadron reached a major milestone on 28 August when it flew its 2000th combat mission, 496 of which were credited to the second front team. By this time the unit had accounted for 183 confirmed kills, with 26 credited to the newcomers. The most successful were rotnik Anton Matusek with 12 victories, catnik Alexander Geric with eight and nadporucik Juraj Puskar with three. The Slovak pilots received congratulatory signals not only from the CO of *I. Fliegerkorps*, Generalleutnant Carl Angerstein, but also from 17th Army CO Generaloberst Erwin Jaenecke.

DESERTIONS

There was no time for the Slovaks to rest on their laurels. The Axis forces in Kuban came under pressure as the Red Army advanced and forced a retreat from the Kuban bridgehead. In the altered military situation No 13 Sqn suffered several defections of flying and ground personnel.

Few Slovak soldiers and airmen went to the eastern front with great enthusiasm. Indeed, war with the Soviet Union was not popular among the Slovak people in the summer of 1941, and was even less so two years later when the military situation of their German ally deteriorated. It made no difference that the atheist Communist philosophy was in direct opposition to the deeply religious feelings of the Slovaks. In fact these feelings were suppressed by sympathy for fellow Slavs. Like the Croats, the Slovaks objected to some aspects of their treatment by the Germans, who did not always behave as allies, and this had an adverse affect on many personnel in the field.

The Bf 109G-4/R6 was known in service as the *Kanonenboot* (Gunboat). Pictured here with an example operated by 13(*slow*)./ JG 52 at Anapa in the summer of 1943 are, from left to right, catnik Alexander Geric and rotniks Gustav Kubovic, Anton Matusek and Frantisek Melichac. Matusek and Geric were both aces with twelve and nine victories respectively, and in September 1943 they flew their *Gustavs* over to the Soviets (*K Geletko*)

Even so, in March 1943 the chief of the air department of the *Deutsche Luftwaffenmission in der Slowakei*, Oberstleutnant Ignacius Weh, felt able to report after a tour of inspection that 'the Slovak fighter squadron is delighted to fight'. His remarks, however, referred only to the first front team, which was highly commended by its German superiors.

In the changed situation on the eastern front, their successors seemed less enthusiastic. This was noticed by the Germans, and Major Dietrich Hrabak, JG 52's *Geschwaderkommodore*, and Hauptmann Gerhard Barkhorn, II./JG 52's *Gruppenkommandeur*, felt obliged to watch how the Slovak pilots performed their allotted tasks in the air. Morale was not aided when the men were served goulash made from cats! But above all, the Slovak squadron resented being abandoned at the Kuban bridgehead with only a small German staff after five Luftwaffe units were withdrawn.

The first results came in September 1943, when rotnik Anton Matusek and catniks Ludovit Dobrovodsky and Alexander Geric flew their *Gustavs*

Formerly used by Reznak, Bf 109G-4 Wk-Nr 19347 'Yellow 9' was flown over to the Soviets by Anton Matusek on 9 September 1943. Matusek later flew Lavochkin La-5FNs with the 1st Czechoslovak Fighter Air Regiment, but the fate of his *Gustav* is unknown (*via J Bobek*)

over to the Soviet side. Although the Soviets ascribed these defections to pro-Communist feelings, it is likely that the pilots' motives were rather more complicated. Matusek and Geric were the most successful pilots of the second front team with twelve and nine kills respectively, while Dobrovodsky had one. Although pro-Soviet or pro-Russian sympathies cannot be ruled out, Matusek and Geric may have wanted to escape punishment for disciplinary violations, and Dobrovodsky may simply have emulated the older and more experienced Matusek, whom he greatly admired.

Whatever their reasons, the fact is that on 9 September 1943 Matusek (in Bf 109G-4 Wk-Nr 19347 'Yellow 9') and Dobrovodsky (in Bf 109G-4 Wk-Nr 16259 'Yellow 13') took off from Anapa at 1335 hrs to escort a reconnaissance Fw 189 from Kerch. But when their charge did not appear at the rendezvous point after they had circled the port of Temryuk for ten minutes, both fighters headed east and crossed the Soviet lines at low level. They had intended to land at Timashevskaya airfield, but the local defences forced them down in a field near Novomalorossiyskaya. With their undamaged aircraft, they reported to Soviet officials.

Catnik Alexander Geric followed two days later. He and rotnik Stefan Martis were also briefed to escort an Fw 189, but they encountered six Soviet Spitfire Mk VBs east of Novorossiysk. Geric pretended to be hit and defected. Martis returned to Anapa alone, reporting that Geric had been shot down. He also claimed the destruction of one Spitfire, but due to lack of corroboration was not credited with the kill. Meanwhile Geric had landed with his Bf 109G-4 Wk-Nr 14938 'Yellow 2' intact at the Soviet airfield Timashevskaya. He even brought with him radio mechanic slobodnik Vincec Tkacik, who had been trained on the new FuG 17.

Geric and Tkacik were assigned intelligence tasks by the Red Army. On the night of 29-30 June 1944 they parachuted into Slovakia, while Matusek and Dobrovodsky became members of the 1st Czechoslovak Fighter Air Regiment, flying the Lavochkin La-5FN and fighting in the Slovak National Uprising.

When flying over the eastern front, 12-victory ace Anton Matusek flew an aircraft displaying black crosses but returned to his native country at the control of a machine with red stars. After the war he served with the newly-formed Czechoslovakian Air Force until 1948 (*via S Androvic*)

Alexander Geric was recruited by the Soviets after changing sides on 11 September 1943. On the night of 29/30 June 1944 he parachuted into the Trencin area of western Slovakia on an intelligence mission for the Red Army. On 29 August 1944, immediately after the German invasion of Slovakia, he took off from Piestany at the controls of a Praga E-39 biplane trainer but crashed fatally in bad visibility near Puchov (*K Geletko*)

Nadporucik Juraj Puskar (five kills) was the last 13(*slow*)./JG 52 pilot to be shot down in air combat on the eastern front. He is pictured here (right) walking away from Bf 109G-4 'Yellow 1' at Kertch in the autumn of 1943 with, from left to right, rotniks Stefan Ocvirk, Stefan Jambor (in hat) and Robert Nerad (chief mechanic) and squadron CO stotnik Jozef Palenicek also in the photograph. Puskar was shot down by marauding Soviet fighters soon after departing Bagerovo on 19 October 1943. He successfully baled out of his burning Bf 109G-4 Wk-Nr 19248 *Marta*

As the possibility of further defections could not be excluded, stotnik Palenicek asked the Slovak MNO for the squadron's immediate withdrawal to Slovakia, but the Germans had no replacement available. Following the Soviet advance, 13(*slow*)./JG 52 ended the retreat from Anapa on 18 September 1943 at Taman, where it faced superior enemy forces from the reduced area of the Kuban bridgehead. On 24 September the squadron achieved its 200th kill when catnik Rudolf Palaticky shot down two Il-2 *Stormoviks* during a single combat. The second, downed at 1000 hrs over Black Sea, near Taman, became the 200th victory.

Squadron morale revived somewhat on the 27th when it was ordered to move to Kerch, in the Crimea, from what had become the last Axis outpost in Kuban. This move helped ease the parlous supply situation, thus further strengthening morale. The defections stopped.

But the sojourn in Kerch was to be a brief one, for on 12 October the unit moved again, this time to Bagerovo airfield, west of Kerch. Although relief was coming closer for the exhausted Slovak fighters, the squadron's deputy CO, nadporucnik Juraj Puskar (five kills), had a lucky escape on 19 October 1943. Soon after taking off from Bagerovo in Bf 109G-4 Wk-Nr 19248, he was bounced by Soviet fighters. He was shot down and his aircraft burned out after hitting the ground in the Fontana-Mariental area. Puskar, who had taken to his parachute, emerged unhurt.

The last Slovak kill on the eastern front was achieved a week later by rotnik Frantisek Hanovec when, on the 27th, he sent an La-5 into the Kerch Channel. He had been both the first and the last member of the second front team to score a confirmed kill.

The eagerly-awaited departure from the front came the next day when the Slovak pilots handed their Bf 109G-4s over to the Germans and Croatians and headed home by train, arriving on 12 November 1943.

During its four months at the front, the second team had flown approximately 1100 operational sorties and scored 61 confirmed kills, with further 13 unconfirmed. Three pilots were recorded as lost – although they had actually defected – and another two were injured. The combined score achieved by 13(*slow*)./JG 52 in 12 months' fighting rose to 2600 combat sorties and 215 confirmed kills, plus 29 unconfirmed. No fewer than 17 of the 29 pilots sent into action had become aces.

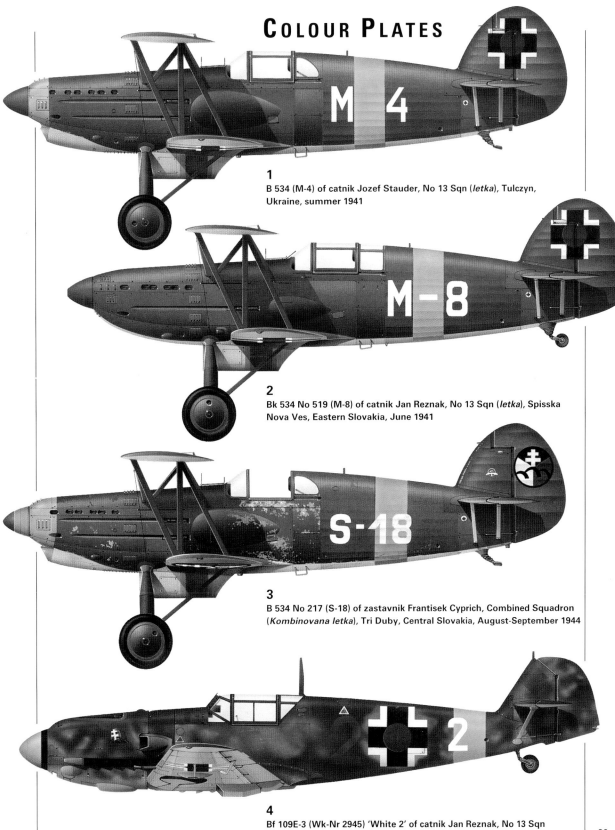

1
B 534 (M-4) of catnik Jozef Stauder, No 13 Sqn (*letka*), Tulczyn, Ukraine, summer 1941

2
Bk 534 No 519 (M-8) of catnik Jan Reznak, No 13 Sqn (*letka*), Spisska Nova Ves, Eastern Slovakia, June 1941

3
B 534 No 217 (S-18) of zastavnik Frantisek Cyprich, Combined Squadron (*Kombinovana letka*), Tri Duby, Central Slovakia, August-September 1944

4
Bf 109E-3 (Wk-Nr 2945) 'White 2' of catnik Jan Reznak, No 13 Sqn (*letka*), Piestany, Slovakia, October 1942

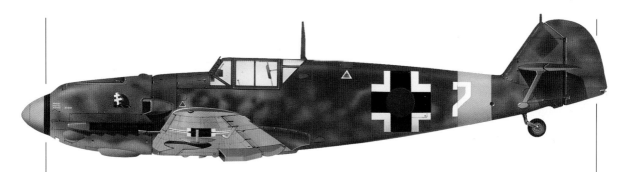

5
Bf 109E-4 (Wk-Nr 3317) 'White 7' of catnik Stefan Martis, No 13 Sqn, Piestany, Slovakia, October 1942

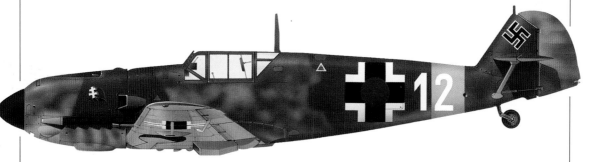

6
Bf 109E-7 (Wk-Nr 6474) 'White 12' of porucik Vladimir Krisko, 13(*slow*)./JG 52, Maikop, Kuban, November 1942

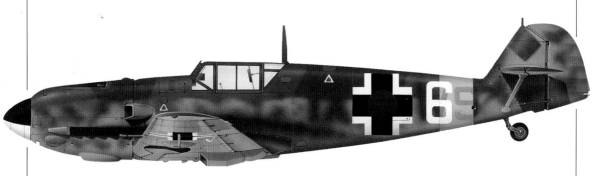

7
Bf 109E-7 (Wk-Nr 6476) 'White 6' of catnik Jan Reznak, 13(*slow*)./JG 52, Maikop, Kuban, November 1942

8
Bf 109E-4 'White 1' of zastavnik Frantisek Brezina, No 13 Sqn, Vajnory, Slovakia, September 1943

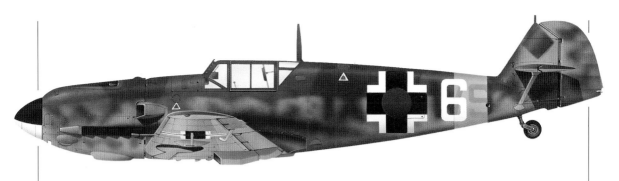

9
Bf 109E-4 (Wk-Nr 2787) of rotnik Stefan Ocvirk, Combined Squadron (*Kombinovana letka*), Tri Duby, Slovakia, October 1944

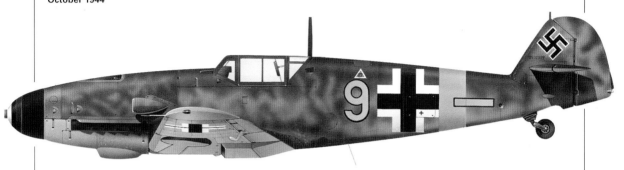

10
Bf 109G-4 (Wk-Nr 19347) 'Yellow 9' of rotnik Jan Reznak, 13(*slow*)./JG 52, Anapa, Kuban, April-May 1943

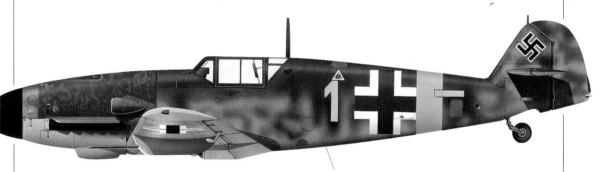

11
Bf 109G-2/R6 'Yellow 1' of rotnik Izidor Kovarik, 13(*slow*)./JG 52, Anapa, Kuban, April-May 1943

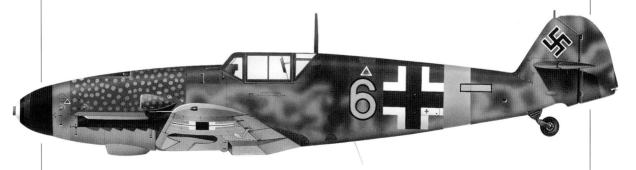

12
Bf 109G-4 (Wk-Nr 19330) 'Yellow 6' of rotnik Jan Reznak, 13(*slow*)./JG 52, Anapa, Kuban, April-May 1943

13
Bf 109G-4/R6 CU+PQ of rotnik Frantisek Brezina, 13(*slow*)./JG 52, Anapa, Kuban, April 1943

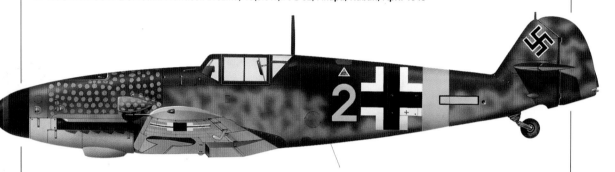

14
Bf 109G-4 'Yellow 2' of nadporucik Jan Gerthofer, 13(*slow*)./JG 52, Anapa, Kuban, April 1943

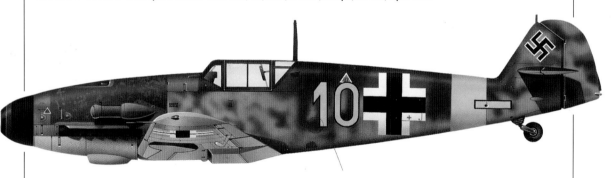

15
Bf 109G-4/Trop (probably Wk-Nr 15195) 'Yellow 10' of rotnik Stefan Martis, 13(*slow*)/JG 52, Anapa, Kuban, September 1943

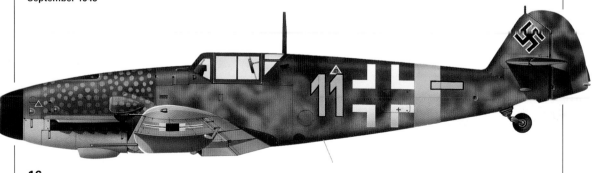

16
Bf 109G-4/R6 'Yellow 11' of nadporucik Jan Gerthofer, 13(*slow*)./JG 52, Anapa, Kuban, May 1943

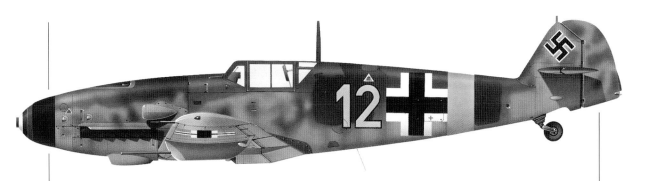

17
Bf 109G-4/R6 (Wk-Nr 19543) 'Yellow 12' of nadporucik Vladimir Krisko, 13(*slow*)./JG 52, Anapa, Kuban, April 1943

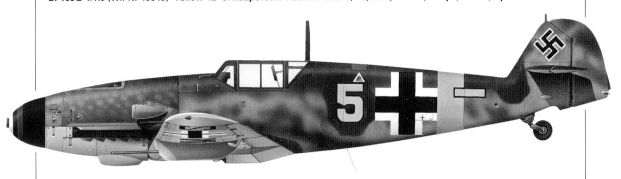

18
Bf 109G-4/R6 (Wk-Nr 14761) 'Yellow 5' of catnik Rudolf Bozik, 13(*slow*)./JG 52, Anapa, Kuban, September 1943

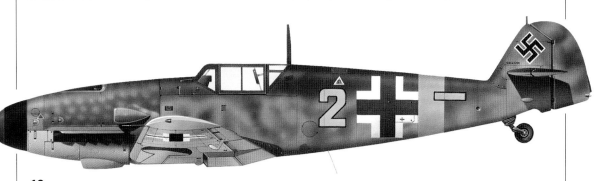

19
Bf 109G-4 (Wk-Nr 14938) 'Yellow 2' of catnik Alexander Geric, 13(*slow*)./JG 52, Anapa, Kuban, September 1943

20
Bf 109G-6 (Wk-Nr 161722) 'White 1' of zastavnik Jozef Stauder,
No 13 Sqn (*letka*), Plestany, Slovakla, June 1944

21
Bf 109G-6 (Wk-Nr 161720) 'White 3' of nadporucik Juraj Puskar, No 13 Sqn (*letka*), Piestany, Slovakia, June 1944

22
Bf 109G-6 (Wk-Nr 161728) 'White 2' of zastavnik Jozef Stauder, No 13 Sqn (*letka*), Piestany, Slovakia, June 1944

23
Bf 109G-6 (Wk-Nr 161717) 'White 6' of zastavnik Pavel Zelenak, No 13 Sqn (*letka*), Piestany, Slovakia, June 1944

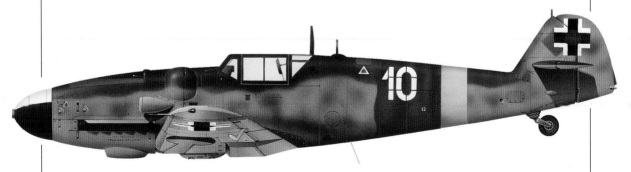

24
Bf 109G-6 (Wk-Nr 161713) 'White 10' of rotnik Frantisek Hanovec, No 13 Sqn (*letka*), Piestany, Slovakia, June 1944

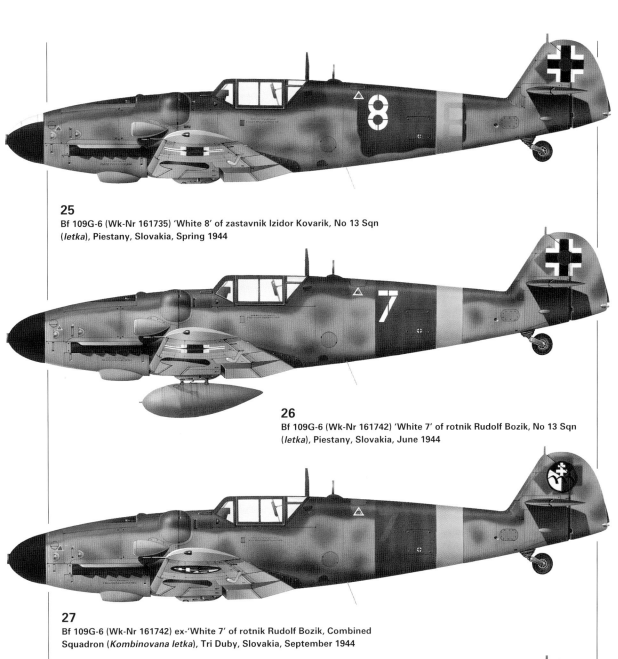

25
Bf 109G-6 (Wk-Nr 161735) 'White 8' of zastavnik Izidor Kovarik, No 13 Sqn
(*letka*), Piestany, Slovakia, Spring 1944

26
Bf 109G-6 (Wk-Nr 161742) 'White 7' of rotnik Rudolf Bozik, No 13 Sqn
(*letka*), Piestany, Slovakia, June 1944

27
Bf 109G-6 (Wk-Nr 161742) ex-'White 7' of rotnik Rudolf Bozik, Combined
Squadron (*Kombinovana letka*), Tri Duby, Slovakia, September 1944

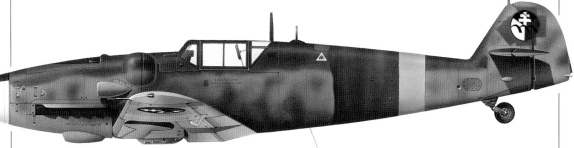

28
Bf 109G-6 (Wk-Nr 161725) of stabni rotmistr Frantisek Cyprich, Combined Squadron
(*Kombinovana letka*), Tri Duby, Slovakia, September 1944

29
La-5FN 'White 62' of stabni rotmistr Anton Matusek, 1st Czechoslovak Fighter Air Regiment
(1. *ceskoslovensky stihaci letecky pluk*), Zolna and Tri Duby, Slovakia, September 1944

30
La-7 (serial number 45210806) 'White 06' of *Gorkovskiy rabochiy*, 2nd Czechoslovak Fighter Air Regiment
(2. *ceskoslovensky stihaci letecky pluk*), Prague, May-June 1945

31
La-7 (probably serial number 45212611) 'White 11' of rotmistr Stefan Ocvirk, 2nd Air Regiment (*Letecky pluk* 2), Piestany,
Slovakia, July 1946

32
B 135 of kapitan Krastyo Atanasov, CO of the Bulgarian Fighter Pilots' School, Dolna Mitropoliya, Bulgaria, 30 March 1944

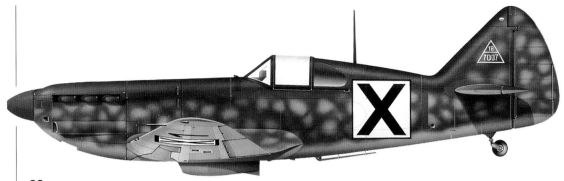

33
D.520 'Red 1' of poruchik Assen Kovatchev, CO of the 662nd *Yato*, 2.6 *Orlyak*, Vrazhdebna, Bulgaria,
December 1943-January 1944

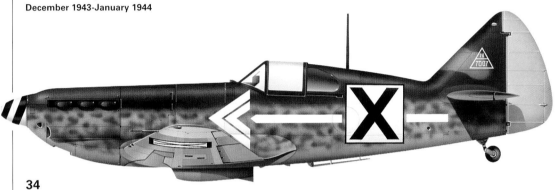

34
D.520 of an unidentified Bulgarian unit, Karlovo, Bulgaria, 1943-44

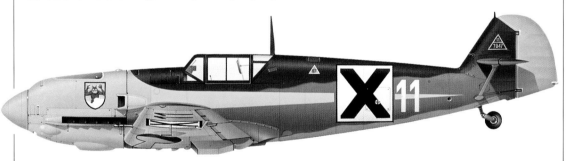

35
Bf 109E-4 'White 11' of Mikhail Grigorov, CO of the 672nd *Yato*, 3.6 *Orlyak*, Karlovo, Bulgaria, early 1943

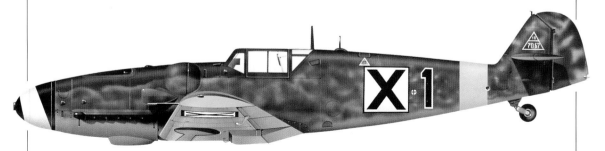

36
Bf 109G-6 'Black 1'of Stoyan Stoyanov, CO of the 682nd *Yato*, 3.6 *Orlyak*, Bozhurishte, Bulgaria, early 1944

37
Bf 109G-6 'Red 6' of podporuchik S Marinopolski, 652nd *Yato*, 2.6 *Orlyak*, Vrazhdebna, Bulgaria, December 1943

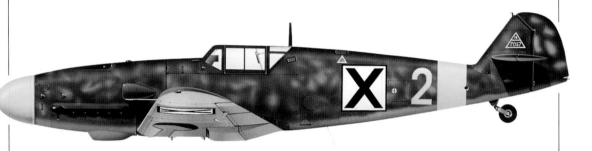

38
Bf 109G-2 'Yellow 2' of poruchik Ditmar Spisarevski, 3.6 *Orlyak*, Karlovo, Bulgaria, 20 December 1943

39
Bf 109G-6 'White 7' of poruchik Somov, 3.6 *Orlyak*, Bozhurishte, Bulgaria, Summer 1944

IN SLOVAKIAN SKIES

As soon as it became clear that Slovakian airspace was being menaced by USAAF units stationed in southern Italy, the Ministry of National Defence was forced to consider anti-aircraft defences. Accordingly, on 20 August 1943 a four-aircraft emergency formation controlled by a readiness unit was established at Vajnory airport in Bratislava. Initially, it comprised four Bf 109Es – E-2s, E-4s and E-7s – and a Praga E 39 liaison aircraft. Later, an S 328 and a B 534 were added.

The first pilots assigned to the unit were rotniks Frantisek Cyprich, Izidor Kovarik, Jan Reznak, Frantisek Brezina, Pavel Zelenak and Jozef Stauder. All were aces, and members of the No 13 Sqn first front team in the east. Cyprich initially served as CO, although he was relieved on 8 November 1943 by Vladimir Krisko.

Reinforcements arrived after several months in the shape of the second front team, which had just returned from the eastern front, and new equipment purchased from Germany. This influx and men and machines allowed the small emergency formation to be supplanted by the whole of No 13 Sqn, which was formally given the role of defending Slovakia on 31 January 1944. From then on, the unit was known as the Readiness

Four Bf 109Es are seen sat side-by-side at Vajnory in the summer of 1943. These now obsolete fighters are, from top to bottom, E-2 Wk-Nr 972, E-4 Wk-Nr 3317 and E-7s Wk-Nrs 4870 and 6442. They all belong to a readiness unit intended to defend the Slovak capital, Bratislava, and the Povazi Valley industrial zone. The aircraft display recognisable traces of the original over-painted German radio codes (*via J Rajninec*)

Now members of the readiness unit assigned to defend Slovakian airspace, six veteran 13(*slow*)./JG 52 eastern front aces pose for the camera at Vajnory in the late summer of 1943. They are, from left to right, zastavniks Pavel Zelenak (12 kills), Frantisek Cyprich (12 kills), Izidor Kovarik (28 kills), Frantisek Brezina (14 kills), Jozef Stauder (12 kills) and Jan Reznak (32 kills). Behind them stand obsolete *Emils*

This readiness unit Bf 109E-4, seen at Vajnory in the autumn of 1943, was flown by many aces, including zastavnik Frantisek Brezina (14 kills) (*K Geletko*)

The Readiness Squadron was re-equipped with 15 Bf 109G-6s, delivered from the Messerschmitt AG factory at Regensburg, in early 1944. Zastavnik Jan Reznak stands in front of one of the new arrivals at Piestany in the spring of that year (*via S Androvic*)

Bf 109G-6 Wk-Nr 161735 'White 8' was one of several Slovakian *Gustavs* which crashed prior to seeing combat. Rotnik Karol Geletko (one eastern front kill) suffered a landing accident when he returned to Spisska Nova Ves aerodrome on 14 June 1944. During his SVZ service, Geletko wrote off no fewer than four *Gustavs* – Bf 109G-4 Wk-Nr 14982 (on 29 September 1943 at Kertch), Bf 109G-6 Wk-Nr 161735 (on 14 June 1944 at Spisska Nova Ves), Bf 109G-6 Wk-Nr 161722 (on 3 August 1944 at Isla) and Bf 109G-6 Wk-Nr 161741 (on 17 August 1944 at Isla) (*K Geletko*)

Squadron. It was staffed by 18 pilots under the command of Krisko, with nadporucnik Juraj Puskar as his deputy. Both men were eastern front aces with nine and five kills respectively.

When No 13 Sqn returned from the eastern front, it had been obliged to leave its Bf 109G-4s behind. Although it now had 14 aircraft – two Bf 109E-1s, an E-2, an E-3, six E-4s, an E-7, two B 534s and a Bk 534 – they were not up to the task of defending Slovakian airspace against high-flying USAAF bombers, and their fighter escorts. As a result, 15 Bf 109G-6s were acquired from Germany, and all but one of these was flown by Slovak pilots from Regensburg to Piestany on 11 February 1944. The 15th machine was damaged en route and delivered by rail.

Increasing Allied air activity in the Central European theatre soon raised the possibility of clashes with Slovak fighters. This finally happened on 13 April when experienced Frantisek Hanovec and Rudolf Bozik (wingman) were scrambled towards Slovakia's southern borders. They were, however, flying the older *Emils,* and this was to have unforeseen consequences.

Nearing the border, Bozik spotted an unknown aircraft in front of him and started closing on it. At first he took its twin fins and rudders to indicate a four-engined American B-24 Liberator bomber. He realised his error when he caught up with aircraft. It was actually a Bf 110G-2 (Wk-Nr 6397 2N+HM) twin-engined fighter, whose large ventral fuel tanks and twin fins and rudders had made it look like a B-24 from a distance. But just as Bozik was about to break away, the Bf 110's gunner opened fire. Bozik returned fire and the aircraft crashed near Podunajske Biskupice at 1230 hrs. The rear gunner managed to bale out but the pilot, Leutnant Wilhelm Meilinger of II./ZG 1, based at Wels, in Austria, was killed.

Slovakian top scorers zastavniks Jan Reznak and Izidor Kovarik discuss a combat soon after both had been awarded the German Cross in Gold (*Deutsches Kreuz in Gold*) by the chief of the *Deutsche Luftwaffenmission in der Slowakei*, Generalleutnant Ludwig Keiper, in Bratislava on 25 April 1944

When he landed, Bozik reported that he had shot down an American four-engined bomber, and he was backed up in this claim by Hanovec. This appeared to be conformed by the surviving member of the Bf 110's crew, who said his aircraft had been shot down by an American P-51 Mustang! According to his statement, the attacking fighter aircraft had squared-off wing tips like the Bf 109's.

During spring 1944, Slovak *Gustavs* made almost daily sorties against huge American bomber formations but, according to secret instructions, their pilots were to save themselves for an anti-German uprising planned by the Minister of National Defence, Gen Ferdinand Catlos, and the Chief of Staff of the Land Forces, podplukovnik Jan Golian. The latter was a member of the illegal Military Centre, had links with the exiled Czechoslovak government in London.

The difficulty of obeying such an order is well illustrated by the events of 16 June 1944, when Bratislava was attacked for the first time by USAAF bombers. The raid caused major material damage and great loss of life – 717 dead or missing and 592 injured. Although there were fierce fights over Hungary, Austria and southern Slovakia, with losses on both sides, six Slovak *Gustavs* which had taken off from Piestany at 0920 hrs failed to intercept the bombers. Circling high above Bratislava, their pilots were interested only in the large column of smoke and fire rising from the Slovak capital. Anti-aircraft gunners, however, shot down two American aircraft.

The Slovak fighter pilots' passive response drew sharp criticism. Officers of *Deutsche Luftwaffenmission in der Slowakei* accused five-victory ace nadporucik Juraj Puskar of cowardice. He had been leading No 13 Sqn at the time, as squadron CO Krisko was sick. Similar accusations were made by the civilians of Piestany, who had close links with the airmen based there. This was to

Readiness Squadron deputy CO nadporucik Juraj Puskar was an eastern front veteran, having shot down three Airacobras and two *Stormoviks* in the summer of 1943. He led the Slovakian fighters which intercepted a USAAF bomber formation on 26 June 1944, Puskar's Bf 109G-6 Wk-Nr 161720 'White 3' falling victim to escorting Mustangs and crashing between Brestovany and Lovcice

lead to tragedy, and the disbandment of the Readiness Squadron just a few days later.

On the morning of 26 June 1944, another huge formation of USAAF bombers droned towards the Slovak borders. It comprised 501 B-24 Liberators and 154 B-17 Flying Fortresses, escorted by 290 P-38 Lightnings and P-51 Mustangs. Their targets were oil refineries and depots around Vienna. In all, 203 German, 30 Hungarian and eight Slovak fighters scrambled to intercept the formation in what would be the biggest encounter between American and Axis air forces over Slovakian territory.

The eight Slovak *Gustavs* took off from Piestany at 0840 hrs in four two-aircraft sections, each machine being flown by an experienced eastern front veteran from 13(*slow*)./JG 52. Now they were to encounter a far more dangerous foe. Juraj Puskar was anxious to dispel the notion that the 'Tatra Eagles' were cowards, and prior to taking off, he told his pilots 'Today we attack'. His plan was simple – perform an 'exhibition' attack on a group of American bombers and then depart quickly. At 13,000 ft (4000 m) he ordered his pilots to don their oxygen masks, and when they reached 30,000 ft (9500 m), flying in loose formation, he ordered them to drop their external fuel tanks and attack. The Slovaks were overwhelmed by a superior number of American fighters, however, and it was all over in a few minutes.

Only rotnik Gustav Lang, flying Wk-Nr 161713 'White 10', succeeded in shooting down an American aircraft. He attacked lone B-24H 41-28674, flown by 2Lt Lincoln E Artz, of the 758th Bombardment Squadron, 459th Bombardment Group. The nine crewmembers managed to bale out of the stricken bomber, which crashed at Most na Ostrove. Some were captured in Slovak territory and the rest on the Hungarian side of the border.

The American escort fighters literally swept the Slovak interceptors from the skies. As Lang was breaking away from his victim, Lightnings riddled his aircraft with gunfire and he was badly wounded. He died when his aircraft crashed near Miloslavice na Ostrove. Puskar's 'White 3' (Wk-Nr 161720) fell victim to three Mustangs and crashed between the villages of Brestovany and Horne Lovcice. Rotnik Stefan Jambor was the third to die, also hunted down by Mustangs. His burning 'White 4' (Wk-Nr 161723) crashed on Hungarian territory between Hubice and

Bf 109G-6 Wk-Nr 161717 'White 6' was another victim of the 26 June 1944 massacre at the hands of USAAF fighters. Zastavnik Pavol Zelenak (12 kills) was attacked by 11 Lightnings which followed him as he dived to escape. Eight of them eventually gave up the chase, but three pursued Zelenak as he tried to land at Piestany off a straight-in approach. He had to go around for a second try, enabling the P-38s to score hits on his cockpit, wounding Zelenak in the head and hands. He was able to belly-land his machine at high speed near Brunovce. Although badly injured, Zelenak survived the war (*via S Spurny*)

His active career as a pilot over following the 26 June 1944 incident, Pavel Zelenak served with the Czechoslovak Air Force in various ground posts after the war. He finally left the service in 1958

Zastavnik Jozef Stauder (12 kills), was one of the luckier Slovakian pilots involved in the attempted interception of USAAF bombers on 26 June 1944. His Bf 109G-6 Wk-Nr 161728 'White 2' was hit in the radiator and engine by the Mustang escorts, starting a fire. Stauder tried to extinguish the flames by diving, and was partially successful, but he nevertheless had to belly-land his fighter at Ivanka pri Dunaji. The ace emerged unhurt (*via M Krajci*)

Jozef Stauder claimed 12 victories with 13(*slow*)./JG 52 on the Eastern Front during 1943. After the war, he rejoined the Czechoslovak Air Force, serving as an officer until 1958 (*via S Androvic*)

Stvrtok na Ostrove. The pilot's body was found near the wreckage. According to some reports, he was machine-gunned while hanging helplessly in his parachute, but others state that his parachute became detached and he fell to his death.

The drama was not yet over. Zastavnik Pavel Zelenak (12 kills) tried to escape to Piestany but was pursued down to ground level by 11 Lightnings. His 'White 6' (Wk-Nr 161717) was hit by a cannon shell, and during the ensuing belly landing at Brunovce, he was wounded by shell splinters which broke his backbone.

Zastavnik Jozef Stauder (12 kills) was considerably luckier. His 'White 2' (Wk-Nr 161728) was hit in the engine and radiator by Mustangs, but he still managed to belly land at Ivanka pri Dunaji without injury. Rotnik Ocvirk (five kills) brought 'White 5' (Wk-Nr 161718) back to Piestany, but with its hydraulic system damaged by gunfire from two Mustangs, he was also forced to belly land. Rotnik Rudolf Bozik (nine kills) found himself in a similar position. With his 'White 7' (Wk-Nr 161742) hit by fire from Flying Fortress gunners, he managed to reach Piestany uninjured. Rotnik Karel Geletko, flying as Lang's wingman, escaped pursuing Lightnings by flinging his 'White 8' (Wk-Nr 161741) into in a steep dive. His was the only undamaged machine to return home.

The 'exhibition' attack had left three pilots dead and one grievously wounded, while eight of the aircraft sortied had been written off. The Slovak fighter pilots may have demonstrated their courage, but as a serviceable unit, the Readiness Squadron had virtually ceased to exist.

At that time the eastern front was rolling ever nearer to Slovakia, where revolution was fomenting with the aim of avoiding the fate of a defeated ally, which Nazi Germany must surely be. The East Slovakian Corps, comprising the 1st and 2nd Infantry Divisions under the command of Gen Augustin Malar, was hastily sent to defend the country's now-threatened eastern borders.

The badly-holed Bf 109G-6 Wk-Nr 161741 'White 5', flown by rotnik Stefan Ocvirk (five kills), is seen in the aftermath of the 26 June 1944 combat with US fighters. Flying as Puskar's wingman, Ocvirk was attacked by two Mustangs and received hits in the wing. He immediately threw his Bf 109 into a tight spin and succeeded in shaking off his pursuers. Ocvirk made it back to base, where he performed a textbook belly-landing after he discovered that his hydraulic system had been damaged. The ace was exhausted, but unhurt, and his aircraft was later repaired (*via S Androvic*)

The funeral of the three Slovakian pilots killed in combat with American fighters on 26 June 1944 took place in Piestany three days after they had fallen. The remains of Puskar, Jambor and Lang were then taken to their native towns for burial

SVZ top scorer zastavnik Jan Reznak is seen during the funeral service. He carries the awards and decorations of one of his fallen comrades – probably those of rotnik Gustav Lang

According to the plans of the German *Heeresgruppe Nord-Ukraine*, this Corps, which included 90 per cent of the Slovak armed forces stationed at home, was supposed to defend the Carpathian passes. The leaders of the planned *coup d'etat* had other ideas, for they wanted to open the passes to the Red Army so that it could rapidly occupy the country. Air defence of the Corps was entrusted to the newly-formed Air Arms Group (*Skupina vzdusnych zbrani*), which comprised single fighter, observation and reconnaissance squadrons. They were equipped with 42 aircraft of various types (including 28 combat machines) and manned by more than 550 men, 57 of whom were pilots. The group, which moved to East Slovakia between 27 July to 3 August 1944, was led by Maj Julius Trnka.

This unit now had the best machines available to the Slovak Air Arms, the obsolete aircraft remaining well behind the frontlines, mainly at Tri Duby airfield, in Central Slovakia, where a flying school was based.

The group's fighter force was formed by No 12 Sqn under the command of stotnik Jozef Palenicek. On 2 August 1944 it moved from Spisska Nova Ves to Isla with five B 534s and one Bk 534, together with an E 39 and a Fi 156C-3 Storch as liaison aircraft. The unit was reinforced by four Bf 109G-6s which had remained airworthy with the Readiness Squadron at Piestany after the encounter with the Americans on 26 June 1944. On 1 August these machines were flown to Isla by rotniks Rudolf Bozik (nine kills), Frantisek Hanovec (six), Rudolf Palaticky (six) and Karol Geletko (one).

The Germans were expecting the East Slovakian Corps to fail in its mission, so at the end of August 1944 they carried out operation *Kartoffel-ernte mit Prämie* to disarm them and intern their personnel. Many airmen to flew to the Soviet Union in an effort to avoid disarmament, some 81 machines (including three B 534s, a Bk 534 and the only two airworthy Bf 109G-6s) fleeing eastwards on 31 August. All the Slovakian aircraft made a landing of one sort or another in Lvov (Lemberg), which was occupied by the Red Army. The Slovak Air Arms had lost its best men and machines. Deprived of contact with home, the airmen were unaware that the uprising, centred on Banska Bystrica and Tri Duby, had broken out on the 29th. The Air Arms Group would have represented a significant reinforcement for the uprising at Tri Duby had they stayed in Slovakia.

NATIONAL UPRISING

By the end of August, Bratislava no longer exercised governmental power over Slovakia. This was the main reason why the Slovak neo-fascist government accepted a German offer of military intervention, and invited German units into the country under the pretext of countering the 'partisans'. On the 29th the *Wehrmacht* and the *Waffen* SS Began to occupy the territory of the unreliable Slovak ally from several directions. At the same time the Slovak Army began to show resistance, and the first clashes took place with the advancing German troops.

The Central Slovakian city of Banska Bystrica now became the seat of the uprising. Here too began the legal activity of the Slovak National Council, whose first act was to issue a declaration calling for a new Czechoslovak Republic based on the principle of equality between the Czechs and Slovaks. At the same time, the Council took over legislative and executive power in Slovakia, and declared itself for the Allies and the

Slovak Army as part of the Czechoslovak armed forces fighting alongside the Allies.

The main flying element of the insurgent air force was concentrated at Tri Duby, a major air base between Zvolen and Banska Bystrica. Its CO was Maj Jozef Toth, a former deputy Chief of Staff of the Slovak Air Arms, with Maj Ondrej Dumbala, previously flying school CO, as his deputy. This now became a magnet for Slovak airmen who made there way there, sometimes with their aircraft, from bases housing remnants of the Slovak Air Arms such as Vajnory, Spisska Nova Ves, Trencianske Biskupice, Mokrad, Poprad, Zilina and Piestany.

These obsolete aircraft carried out operational sorties from Tri Duby against the advancing Germans during the first days of the uprising. At the same time, the Combined Squadron (*Kombinovana letka*) was formed under the command of nadporucik Mikulas Singlovic, who was to be succeeded by nine-victory ace nadporucik Vladimir Krisko before the end of the uprising.

Although it had more than 60 aircraft, the Combined Squadron's equipment was mainly obsolete machines used for training, liaison and transport, few of which were suitable for operational use. Initially, it had just four B 534s and two Bf 109E-4s, but without ammunition and spare parts. Personnel, on the other hand, comprised many experienced instructors such as dostojnicky zastupcas Frantisek Brezina (a 14-kill ace from eastern front) and Frantisek Cyprich (12 kills), together with rotnik Stefan Ocvirk (five kills).

From the first days of the uprising, the Combined Squadron protected the airspace, attacked advancing German forces, dropped leaflets and maintained contact with other units. Its aircraft often returned damaged, and sometimes with wounded crews. Groundcrew personnel had their work cut out keeping the aircraft operational. During the uprising – between the end of August and the end of October – the Combined Squadron flew about 350 sorties and dropped 23 tons of bombs. It also shot down six enemy aircraft, including five by fighters (three Fw 189s, two Ju 88s and a Ju 52/3m.

During the first week of the anti-German uprising in September 1944, the only fighters available to the Combined Squadron were two Bf 109E-4s and four B 534s. This particular B 534, displaying insurgent insignia at Tri Duby, was used by former eastern front ace Frantisek Cyprich to down a Hungarian Ju 52/3m transport aircraft on 2 September. His victory is thought to have been the last aerial kill ever scored by a fixed undercarriage biplane (*UDML*)

The first victory for the insurgents was achieved by a veteran of previous Slovak Air Arms campaigns, Frantisek Cyprich. On 2 September, while flying a B 534, he shot down a Ju 52/3m of 102/1 *futarszalito szazad* MKHL (102/1 Transport Squadron of the Royal Hungarian Air Force). The badly damaged tri-motor, which was on its way from Budaors to Cracow with two intelligence officers and mail, was forced to land at Radvan, near Banska Bystrica. Two of the six men on board were killed by Cyprich's fire, while four others, including the injured pilot, Lt Gyorgy Gach, were captured.

'I caught up with him over Radvan', Cyprich later wrote. 'I had him fully in my sights on my first pass. It was as if there was a barn in front of me. All my fire hit him. But I realised I had to do it another way, and in my second pass I aimed at the port engine. Smoke started to come out. After that I aimed at the starboard engine and then I saw him going down. I was glad to have shot down the first aircraft in the uprising, and proudly landed at the airfield.'

It was the last aerial victory achieved by a biplane with a fixed undercarriage in World War 2. But it should be added that Cyprich had all the advantages – the slow and unarmed Junkers, whose crew was unaware of the uprising, was easy meat even for an obsolete B 534 flown by a top Slovak fighter pilot. He received no praise. 'On landing, I reported to nadporucik Singlovic',

Frantisek Cyprich's Hungarian Ju 52/3m was the first aerial victory claimed by the insurgents during the uprising. The tri-motor transport was en route from Budaors, in Hungary, to Cracow, in occupied Poland, when it was intercepted. The crippled machine crashed while attempting to land at Radvan, near Banska Bystrica. Two of the passengers on board the aircraft were killed and four others, including the captain, Lt Gyorgy Gach, were captured. Several days later Cyprich downed a Ju 88 and shared in the destruction of an Fw 189 (*UDML*)

Frantisek Cyprich was probably the only pilot able to claim to have shot down Soviet, German and Hungarian aircraft. He scored a total of 14 and one 1 shared kills, and he was awarded the Slovakian Silver Medal of Military Victory Cross, Silver Military Merit Cross, Silver and Bronze Medal for Heroism, German Eisernkreuz I. and II. Klasse, Croatian Silver Medal of Crown of King Zvonimir, Czechoslovak War Cross, Czechoslovak Medal for Bravery, Order of Slovak National Uprising 1st Class and the Soviet Medal For Victory over Germany. Today, he lives in Trencin, Slovakia (*via M Fekets*)

On 6 September 1944 two Bf 109G-6s (Wk-Nrs 161742 and 161725) were flown back to Slovakia from the Soviet rear areas by rotniks Rudolf Bozik and Frantisek Hanovec in an effort to reinforce the insurgents' Combined Squadron. They were put to use within a few minutes of their arrival at Tri Duby when they shot down an Fw 189 reconnaissance aircraft. Here, Bozik is sitting in the cockpit of Wk-Nr 161742 (formerly 'White 7') in which he survived combat with USAAF fighters on 26 June 1944. While a member of No 13 Sqn, 'Rudo' Bozik scored nine confirmed kills – eight Soviet and (by mistake) one German aircraft claimed as American. As a member of the Combined Squadron, he added two further German aircraft plus one shared with Cyprich (*UDML*)

Frantisek Brezina (14 victories) returns to Tri Duby after completing a sortie over insurgent territory on 7 September 1944. His Bf 109G-6 Wk-Nr 161725 was destroyed on the ground three days later during a Luftwaffe air raid, and the sole remaining Slovakian *Gustav* (Wk-Nr 161742) was lost on 25 October 1944 when Tri Duby was surrounded by German troops. Hastily flown out of the doomed base by rotnik Augustin Kubovic (one eastern front victory), the fighter crashed near the village of Stefanovce, in eastern Slovakia, while heading for Soviet-held territory (*via S Spurny*)

Cyprich recalled, 'but to my surprise, instead of a smile, I saw a hard face and a severe look. His only question, "Why didn't you force him to land?", almost knocked me down. Ashamed, I had to admit that he had been right. An undamaged aircraft would have been of great service, but the pile of metal at Banska Bystrica was of no use to us'.

The number of available aircraft declined rapidly due to combat damage and lack of spare parts, resulting in only a handful of machines being fit for battle on a daily basis. At the beginning of September reinforcements arrived from the Soviet Union when several machines, including two Bf 109G-6s used in desertions on 31 August 1944, returned to Slovakia. The latter were flown by No 13 Sqn aces rotniks Frantisek Hanovec (six and one shared victories) and Rudolf Bozik (nine kills).

The *Gustavs* provided valuable support for the Combined Squadron within a few minutes of their arrival. With Cyprich and Bozik at the controls, both were scrambled from Tri Duby for their first 'insurgent' interception mission, during which they shot down an Fw 189. On the 12th, Cyprich was flying a *Gustav* when he attacked a reconnaissance Ju 88

Ace Rudolf Bozik shot down both Soviet and German aircraft during World War 2. He is pictured here in the cockpit of his Bf 109G-6 Wk-Nr 161742 (formerly 'White 7') at Tri Duby during the September 1944 uprising. Bozik resumed flying after the war with the Czechoslovak Air Force, but crashed in a Klemm Kl 35D trainer on 2 July 1946 and was badly injured. Later, he taught the theory of flight and left active service in 1958 with the rank of stotnik (*UDML*)

Combined Squadron chief-armourer dostojnicky zastupca Karol Duben, stands on the wing of a insurgent Bf 109G-6 Wk-Nr 161725 at Tri Duby on 7 September 1944. Besides being flown by Hanovec and Cyprich, this aircraft was also used by squadron aces Bozik and Brezina. The aircraft was destroyed at Tri Duby in a Luftwaffe air raid three days after this photograph was taken (*UDML*)

and forced the badly damaged German aircraft to land near Brezno nad Hronom. 'The partisans later brought us ammunition stripped from the downed Fw 189 and Ju 88 because we were short', Bozik recalled. Operational activity was limited by a lack of good quality ammunition.

This was the second reconnaissance Ju 88 encountered by Bozik, for on 9 September he had chased down Junkers bomber only for his weapons to malfunction soon after he had caught up with it. His *Gustav* had suffered 28 hits from one of the Ju 88's gunners during the engagement, damaging its hydraulic system and rudder. Lack of spare parts grounded the aircraft permanently, and it was completely destroyed during a Luftwaffe attack on Tri Duby three days later. Bozik had taken off to intercept the raiders in the second *Gustav*, but again his guns jammed. He made simulated attacks on the diving Junkers nonetheless, forcing the German bomber to miss its target.

Bozik's luck improved on the 16th, when he flew the sole *Gustav* in an attack on a lone Ju 88 which caught fire after three passes and crashed into a forest at Nova Bana. On 4 October Bozik achieved the final victory by an insurgent *Gustav* when he chased a reconnaissance Fw 189 and, after three passes, shot it down near Turciansky Svaty Martin.

Finally, the 1st Czechoslovak Fighter Air Regiment, under the command of Staff Captain Frantisek Fajtl (former CO of the RAF's Nos 122 and 313 Sqns), became involved in the Uprising. Twenty of its Lavochkin La-5FN fighters landed at Zolna airstrip, in central Slovakia, on 17 September, and the regiment became the first regular Czechoslovak unit to re-enter its native country. It subsequently operated from Brezno nad Hronom and Tri Duby. This elite unit soon made its presence felt,

On 17 September 1944 the Slovak insurgents were reinforced by the arrival of 20 La-5FN fighters of the 1st Czechoslovak Fighter Air Regiment. Most of the regiment's pilots were Czechs who, until the beginning of 1944, had flown with the RAF. Among them were two Slovaks, dostojnicky zastupca Anton Matusek (12 kills) and rotnik Ludovit Dobrovodsky (one kill), both members of 13(*slow*)./JG 52 who had defected with their aircraft to the Soviets on 9 September 1943. The regiment operated from Zolna, Brezno nad Hronom and finally from Tri Duby, where this photograph was taken (*L Valousek*)

and the Combined Squadron gained a short respite in which to repair its weary aircraft.

Most of the men serving with the Soviet unit were experienced Czech fighter pilots who had previously served in the RAF, but there were also two Slovaks – dostojnicky zastupca Anton Matusek (12 kills) and rotnik Ludovit Dobrovodsky (one kill). They had both defected from 13(*slow*)./JG 52 to the Soviets with their Bf 109G-4s on 9 September 1943, and now became fully involved in the uprising. Dobrovodsky even added to his score with a confirmed Fw 189 kill.

While some of the insurgent airmen were evacuated to the Soviet Union by air prior to the failure of the uprising, the German *Kampfgruppe Schill* advanced so close that Tri Duby had to be abandoned on 25 October. Unserviceable aircraft of the Combined Squadron and the 1st Regiment were destroyed, but the remainder attempted to reach the Soviet lines. On the 27th, Banska Bystrica – the centre of the Slovak uprising – fell and organised military resistance ceased. Members of the insurgent air force remaining in Slovakia fled to their homes or made their way with partisan and ground units to the forests of the Low Tatra (Nizke Tatry) mountains. There, they waged extensive guerrilla warfare during the winter of 1944-45 until the advancing Red Army arrived in the spring.

Slovak airmen of the Air Arms Group, those who had flown to the Soviet side of their own initiative and others who had fought as infantrymen during the uprising formed the basis of the unit now being created under the supervision of the Red Army in Przemysl. The 1st Czechoslovak Mixed

A trio of La-5FN fighters flown by pilots of the 1st Czechoslovak Fighter Air Regiment are seen on patrol shortly after arriving in Slovakia. The unit's experienced pilots quickly achieved air superiority over insurgent territory, destroying 13 German aircraft without suffering a single loss (L Valousek)

Air Division was officially established on 25 January 1945 under the command of podplukovnik Ludvik Budin. After the necessary reinforcement from Soviet sources, the division comprised a headquarters, three air regiments and support units.

After completing their training at Katowice, in Poland, the 1st Fighter Air Regiment (with 32 La-5FN) and the 3rd Ground Attack Regiment (with 33 Il-2/3m *Stormoviks*) were transferred to Poremba airfield, just 12 miles (20 km) from the frontline in Silesia, on 12-13 April. The 2nd Fighter Air Regiment remained at Krakov-Balice with its La-5FNs and La-7s and did not engage in further combats. The first operation was mounted on 14 April when 16 *Stormoviks*, escorted by 18 Lavochkins, attacked a German armoured brigade and field artillery posts near Olza, on the Polish-Czech border. Escorted by the Lavochkins, the ground-attack *Stormoviks* pounded units of the German *Heeresgruppe Mitte* in the Ostrava, Opava and Tesin areas until 2 May. The German air resistance was already so weak that the division's fighters failed to engage a single enemy aircraft.

Following the German capitulation on 8 May 1945, the whole of the division began to concentrate in liberated Czechoslovakia, and between 14 and 25 May it moved to Prague-Letnany airfield. On 1 June there was a flypast at Praha-Letnany in the presence of the president of Czechoslovakia, Dr Edvard Benes, and on 20 July the division cut its ties with the Red Army. Shortly afterwards, on 1 August 1945, it became the 4th Air Division of the newly-formed Czechoslovak Air Force (the remaining four divisions – the 1st, 2nd, 3rd and 6th) of the new air force were formed from Czechoslovak squadrons returning from Britain. Czechs and Slovaks had therefore returned to the point where their ways had parted six years before.

This La-5FN is seen at Przemysl, Galitzia, in January 1945. A small number of Slovak pilots were trained to fly these aircraft, and they later served with the 1st and 2nd Czechoslovak Fighter Air Regiments and the fighter component of the 1st Czechoslovak Mixed Air Division in the USSR. Aces Cyprich, Bozik, Palaticky and Ocvirk flew with these units (*A Droppa*)

TOP THREE SLOVAKIAN ACES

Jan Reznak

The Slovak Air Arms' ranking ace was born on 14 April 1919 in Jablonica. He became an electro-technician up leaving school, and between April and August 1938 took flying lessons with the Slovak Aero Club. Reznak then enlisted in the Czechoslovak Air Force and attended Pilots' School II at Spisska Nova Ves, where he received his basic military training. NCO and fight pilot training followed, and Reznak completed received his wings just as the independent Slovakia was emerging. As a newly-promoted slobodnik, he was assigned to No 13 Sqn at Piestany in December 1939, where he flew B 534 fighters .

Reznak completed first combat tour on the eastern front between June and August 1941, flying 13 sorties over the Ukraine. Air combat with the weakened Soviet Air Force was infrequent, and the future ace managed to experience aerial combat just once during this tour – and his opponent was an aircraft of Slovakia's ally Hungary, rather than a Russian machine! On 29 July 1941 a Fiat CR.42 of 1/3 Fighter Company appeared over Tulczyn airfield, and a three-aircraft Slovak alert force was erroneously scrambled by the German base commander to intercept it. Reznak was the only one able to catch the 'raider', and he opened fire from long range. By this time the two aircraft were approaching the Fiat's base, and anti-aircraft fire forced Reznak to break off. It was clear to him from this first inconclusive encounter that he should have closed in before opening fire.

After retraining on the Bf 109 in Denmark, he returned to the eastern front in October 1942. Reznak saw near continuous action with No 13 Sqn until July 1943, being part of the unit's first front team (designated 13(slow)./JG 52). He scored his first kill on 17 January 1943, but was himself shot down during his next mission later that same day when he was caught over Krasnodar and badly shot up by a superior force

Jan Reznak, Slovakian ace of aces, poses for the camera soon after receiving the German Cross in Gold. In the first half of 1943 he crashed five times, being shot down twice, but still managed to shoot down 32 Soviet aircraft. Today Reznak lives in Piestany, Slovakia, where No 13 Sqn was based (*via S Androvic*)

of LaGG-3s. Despite his fighter having been hit by 60 bullets and three cannon shells, he managed to land Bf 109E-4 Wk-Nr 2787 back at base without injury. Reznak would continue to enjoy such luck in combat.

On 3 February 1943 he was assigned with Kovarik to escort a Ju 52/3m which was due to fly a German general from Slavyanskaya. The airfield surface was deeply rutted, and when Reznak tried to take-off, his *Friedrich's* tyres were damaged. He tried to retract the undercarriage but his speed was too low, his wingtip hit the ground and Bf 109F-4 Wk-Nr 13367 ground-looped and jolted to a standstill. Reznak was unhurt, but just as he was climbing out, Soviet LaGGs and MiGs attacked the airfield. Reznak hid behind his damaged machine, and although a burst of fire hit the Messerschmitt, he remained unhurt.

He pushed his luck again on 15 February 1943 whilst returning to Slavyanskaya from a *Freie Jagd* in Bf 109F-4 Wk-Nr 7088. Just before landing, a German Ju 87D crossed his path, and with great presence of mind he managed to 'jump' over it. In the resulting hard landing the fuselage broke just behind the cockpit, but again Reznak was unhurt.

Two days later he was flying an Arado Ar 66 biplane when its engine failed over the Sea of Azov. Reznak managed to glide down to land on an ice floe, but the aircraft sank soon afterwards and he and his passenger were rescued just in the nick of time by German soldiers in a boat.

He cheated death yet again on 25 March when a Soviet Pe-2 gunner damaged the engine of Reznak's Bf 109G-2 Wk-Nr 13743. The pilot pulled out of the resulting dive and belly-landed in a cotton field about six miles (10 km) south-east of Taman, but the aircraft was written off. Reznak suffered a bumped forehead and contusions to his right shoulder.

During his second tour he flew 194 combat sorties, took part in 36 combats and achieved 32 confirmed kills – 16 LaGG-3s, five I-16s, four I-153s, three MiG-3s, two DB-3s and a single Pe-2 and Yak-1. Another three remained unconfirmed. These successes made him the Slovak Air Arms' most successful fighter pilot of World War 2.

For his outstanding achievements, Reznak received a number of decorations – the Slovakian Silver Medal of Military Victory Cross, the Silver Military Merit Cross, the Gold, Silver and Bronze Medals for Heroism, the German Eisernkreuz I. and II. Klasse, the Ehrenpokal, the Deutsches Kreuz in Gold and the Croatian Silver Medal of the Crown of King Zvonimir. He was also promoted to zastavnik.

Returning to Slovakia, Reznak served with the Readiness Squadron, and although he flew a further 22 air defence sorties, he gained no further victories. He also had another crash, in Fi 156C-3 Storch Wk-Nr 371. It happened on 6 April 1944 on landing at Piestany when, due to jammed rudder pedals, the aircraft nosed over, damaging the propeller and wing. Again Reznak escaped uninjured. He was not involved in the uprising, remaining in German-occupied west Slovakia until the end of the war.

He joined the newly-formed Czechoslovak Air Force, serving with the Flying School in Prostejov until 1948, when he was discharged because of his 'negative attitude towards the peoples' democracy'. Thanks to Gerthofer's intervention, he became a flying club instructor, but his licence was confiscated by the State Security Police in 1951. Reznak then worked as a design engineer and technical inspector, first in Povazska Bystrica and later in Piestany. Retiring in 1979, he lives in Piestany.

Izidor Kovarik fought gallantly on the eastern front and destroyed 28 Soviet aircraft, only to die in his native country while flying a Go 145 biplane trainer (*via M Fekets*)

Izidor Kovarik

Born on 29 March 1917 in Kopcany, Izidor Kovarik was the son of a carpenter. Joining the air force in the late 1930s, he and his great friend Reznak graduated from pilot training together. Assigned to No 11 Sqn in December 1939, Kovarik fought on the eastern front between June and September 1942, when his squadron supported operations against partisans in the Zhitomir and Ovruc areas. He flew eight combat sorties in B 534s during this time, strafing and bombing enemy forces.

Kovarik's second tour in the East began in October 1942 with No 13 Sqn's first front team, but flying Praga E 241 liaison aircraft rather than fighters. He eventually graduated onto the Bf 109E, and soon claimed 28 confirmed kills in combats over the Caucasus and Kuban – nine LaGG-3s, six Yak-1s, six I-16s, two I-153s, two Il-2s and a single MiG-3, DB-3 and Boston. His most successful day came on 29 May 1943 when he shot down four Yak-1s. Kovarik was shot down just once, on 14 March 1943, while returning with Reznak from a ground attack mission during which he had expended all his ammunition. Reznak attacked a formation of DB-3 bombers and shot down one. Kovarik also attacked the Soviet formation to draw some of the defensive fire away from Reznak, despite his magazines being empty. His Bf 109G-2 (Wk-Nr 10473) was hit and he had to force land in a swamp near Akhtanizovskaya. The aircraft was destroyed but he escaped uninjured.

Kovarik received many decorations, including the Slovakian Silver Medal of Military Victory Cross, the Silver Military Merit Cross, the Gold, Silver and Bronze Medals for Heroism, the German Eisernkreuz I. and II. Klasse, the Ehrenpokal and the Deutsches Kreuz in Gold. Like Reznak, he too was promoted to zastavnik.

Upon returning to Slovakia, Kovarik served with the Readiness Squadron until April 1944, when he was transferred as an instructor to the Slovak Air Arms' flying school at Tri Duby. He died on 11 July 1944 shortly before the uprising when, during a training flight, the wing of his Gotha Go 145 biplane broke off for unexplained reasons and the aircraft crashed near Tri Duby. Both Kovarik and his student were killed.

Jan Gerthofer

An experienced pre-war pilot, Jan Gerthofer was born on 27 May 1910 at Lab, near Malacky. He joined the Czechoslovak Air Force in 1927, and when the independent Slovakia was proclaimed, he was serving with the rank of dostojnicky zastupca as a bomber pilot, flying Marcel Bloch MB.200s and Fokker F IXs with No 83 Sqn (part of Air Regiment 5) at Brno, in Moravia.

Gerthofer subsequently served as a test pilot with the Technical Squadron (later Reserve Squadron) at Piestany, before joining No 11 Sqn to fly B 534s. His first assignment to the eastern front came in the summer of 1941, but as a liaison pilot. In September 1941 he was promoted to porucik.

After completing a Bf 109 course in Denmark, Gerthofer became deputy CO of No 13 Sqn's first front team, and fought over the Caucasus, Kuban, the Black Sea and the Sea of Azov from October 1942 through to

Jan Gerthofer began his career as a bomber pilot with the Slovak Air Arms, but later became the third ranking ace with 26 confirmed kills

July 1943. He flew 175 combat sorties, engaging in 36 combats and achieving 26 confirmed kills – eight LaGG-3s, five Il-2s, four I-16, four Yak-1s, two Airacobras and one Boston, Pe-2 and La-5. Five other claims remained unconfirmed. He was the first Slovak pilot to shoot down an Airacobra, which was regarded as a dangerous opponent.

Gerthofer received the Slovakian Gold Medal of Military Victory Cross, the Silver Military Merit Cross, the Silver and Bronze Medals for Heroism, the German Eisernkreuz I. and II. Klasse, the Ehrenpokal, the Croatian Silver Medal of the Crown of King Zvonimir and the Rumanian Gold Virtue Flying Cross. Prior to returning to Slovakia, he was promoted to nadporucik.

On 31 August 1944, Gerthofer flew Gen Augustin Malar in a Junkers W 34 transport from Vajnory to Isla, where both men were taken prisoner by German troops who were disarming Malar's units. Gerthofer was sent to *Stalag XVIIA* PoW camp in Kaisersteinbruch, Austria, and was not released until February 1945.

After the war, he joined the newly-formed Czechoslovak Air Force, serving as Training Squadron CO at Spisska Nova Ves, and later station adjutant at Piestany. In July 1947 Gerthofer became a civil transport pilot, flying Douglas C-47 Skytrains for members of the Slovak National Council (*Slovenska narodna rada*) and the Corps of Commissioners (*Sbor poverenikov*). But in June 1951 he was discharged for political reasons, finding employment as a manual worker, technical controller and planner. He died on 9 August 1991 at Podbrezova.

TARGET SOFIA

The Bf 109 wheeled around in a tight 180-degree turn. Now, over six miles ahead, a line of dots was fast materialising into a formation of huge four-engined bombers. Podporuchik (1Lt) Stoyan Stoyanov of the *Vazdushni Vojski* (Royal Bulgarian Air Force) had just experienced the awesome defensive fire of a USAAF bomber formation. He was determined to make a frontal attack, and as the Bf 109 hurtled towards the bomber formation at full throttle, the closing speed edged passed 600 mph.

The Bf 109's spinner erupted with gunfire and the glazed nose of the leading B-24 dissolved into fragments. The two aircraft were on a collision course, and to avoid ramming the bomber Stoyanov had to climb. At the same time the B-24 pilot pushed his control column forward. The Messerschmitt fighter missed the bomber by less than 20 ft, having riddled its huge fuselage with cannon and machine gun fire as it passed. Minutes later the B-24 crashed. It had just become the first Allied aircraft to be shot down by the Bulgarian fighter force in World War 2. The date was 1 August 1943, and the Liberator formation was returning from an attack on the Rumanian oilfields at Ploesti.

Bulgaria was no stranger to aerial warfare. In fact its pilots had taken part in one of the earliest conflicts ever to involve aircraft. But the country's interest in military aviation dated even further back, to 1892, when a Bulgarian officer took a flight in a French-owned balloon. But it was not until 1906 that an order by the War Ministry saw an aviation detachment assigned to the Army Engineers' Railway Battalion. A dedicated aircraft detachment was later formed, and by the time Bulgaria sided with Greece, Serbia and Montenegro against the Ottoman Empire to start the First Balkan War in October 1912, it boasted 29 aircraft but only 12 qualified pilots, including eight foreigners.

During the ten-week conflict Bulgarian aircraft undertook reconnaissance and observation flights. They also carried out one of the first aerial bombing attacks ever made when the crew of an Albatros biplane dropped small bombs on Adrianople (now Edirne in Turkey), killing or injuring six people. The conflict ended in May 1913, but a month later the Second Balkan War broke out when Bulgaria attacked Serbia. Aircraft played little part in this conflict, which saw Turkey and Rumania fighting on the Serbian side. The following peace treaty saw Bulgaria forced to cede territory, including Macedonia.

The defeat also led to the reorganisation of Bulgarian military aviation, and a state aircraft factory was established, but not opened until 1917. Two years earlier Bulgaria had joined the Central Powers in the hope of regaining its lost territories. Bulgarian air power, however, was still weak and had to be supported by the Kaiser's Germany. In spring 1916 three Fokker E III monoplanes arrived to help defend Sofia. The air war intensified in 1917, by which time the Bulgarians and Germans had 35 aircraft on the Salonika front to oppose about 60 British and French machines. By 1918 the Allies could field 200 aircraft, while the Central

Powers had just 80. Later that year Germany withdrew most of its troops to support its spring offensive on the western front, forcing a weak Bulgaria to seek an armistice.

HARSH TERMS

The peace treaty signed at Neuilly in November 1919 forced harsh terms on the country. In addition to the loss of eight per cent of its pre-war territory, Bulgaria was forbidden to own or build military aircraft for 20 years. There were even restrictions placed on the use of civilian aircraft. Engine power was limited to 180 hp and aircraft could be purchased only from the victorious powers, Britain, France or Italy.

Inevitably, attempts were made to circumvent these restrictions, and a few aircraft were clandestinely saved from destruction to preserve some military potential and maintain a pool of trained pilots. In 1923 Bulgaria ratified the international civil aviation agreement. The following year an aviation directory was formed, and 25 foreign aircraft acquired. In the meantime secret rearmament was in progress, albeit on a modest scale. An indigenous aircraft industry began to evolve with German participation, and a government factory, DAR (*Darzhavna Aeroplanna Rabotilnitsa*), was established at Bozhurishte, seven miles from Sofia. Initially, it turned out copies of proven designs before moving on to original work.

A second factory was established at Kazanlak by the Czech company Aero in 1926, and in 1930 ownership passed to the Italian manufacturer Caproni. The intention had been to produce Italian designs under licence, but in reality it was turning out machines of original design. The aircraft were officially for civil purposes, but they were light, multi-purpose machines whose military potential was clear. In fact they were used extensively for training pilots, observers and gunners. In the mid-1930s tsar Boris III initiated a rearmament policy which virtually ignored the restrictions of the Neuilly Treaty. Then, on 28 July 1935, the war minister officially created the new Bulgarian Air Force (*Vozdushni Voiski*).

NEW AIRCRAFT ARRIVE

In 1936 Hitler supplied the new air arm with 12 Heinkel He 51B fighters and a similar number of He 45 reconnaissance machines. The following year came a dozen Arado Ar 65 fighters, plus 12 obsolete Dornier Do 11 twin-engined bombers. These aircraft were the personal gift of *Reichsmarschall* Hermann Göring to Boris III.

In July 1938 Bulgaria reached agreement with the Balkan League on repealing the armament restrictions so that the *Vozdushni Voiski* could be revealed publicly. Almost simultaneously, Sofia secured a French bank credit for 375 million Francs for the purchase of armaments, including a number of PZL P.24B fighters from Poland. But the *Vozdushni Voiski* received its biggest boost after the German occupation of Czechoslovakia when the Bulgarians received 78 B 534 fighters, as well as bombers, reconnaissance aircraft and trainers from the now disbanded air force.

Despite this substantial addition to its inventory, Bulgaria's air arm was essentially equipped with a motley collection of obsolete aircraft, and the German occupation of Poland caused the supply of P.24B spare parts to virtually dry up. France was unable to meet an order for Bloch 152 fighters, and plans to supplement the 12 Avia B 135s procured in kit form

These Bf 109E-4s were part of a batch of 19 Messerschmitt fighters delivered to Bulgaria in 1940 for operation by the 6th Fighter *Polk*

in 1940 with licence production in Bulgaria fell through. As a result, the 12 Czech monoplanes (which finally arrived in Bulgaria in 1943) were relegated to flying schools, although on one notable occasion they were pressed into operational service. Further aircraft were received from Germany in 1940-41, including 19 Bf 109Es, which boosted the inventory to 580 aircraft. Although the air force's numerical strength appeared impressive on paper, it was still qualitatively second-rate.

At this time the Balkans was becoming a region of special interest to the major powers. On 27 September 1940 Germany, Italy and Japan signed the Tripartite Pact, followed soon after by Hungary, Rumania and Slovakia. Less than a month later the government in Sofia received a note from *Reich* foreign minister Joachim von Ribbentrop requesting Bulgaria to clarify its position in relation to the Axis. Virtually simultaneously came a warning from Britain that close relations with Germany could put Bulgaria at odds with the Empire. The pressure mounted when the USSR also proposed a military pact.

Yet Bulgaria maintained its neutrality until the end of February 1941. By this time 500,000 German troops had been moved to southern Rumania, near the Bulgarian border. On 1 March 1941 Bulgaria signed the Tripartite Pact and the German 12th Army immediately marched into Bulgaria. Although it served as an assembly area for German troops, Bulgaria was not involved in the invasion of Yugoslavia and Greece (Operation *Marita*). Despite bombing raids by British and Yugoslav aircraft, Sofia maintained its neutrality.

The country's position was further complicated by the German attack on the Soviet Union in June 1941. Traditional ties of friendship, combined with the activities of communist activists, resulted in an uprising and civil war. Sofia could delay direct participation in the war against the Soviets, but on 25 November Bulgaria signed the Anti-Comintern Pact. Events now moved quickly. The attack on Pearl Harbor resulted in a US declaration of war against Japan. As a member of the Tripartite Pact,

Bulgaria was obliged to declare war on both the USA and Britain, and duly did so on 13 December 1941. Although the US did not reciprocate until 18 July 1942, the fate of Bulgaria was now sealed.

AIR FORCE STRUCTURE

By 1939 the *Vazdushni Vojski* had established a new structure. As a result the smallest tactical unit was the flight, comprising three or four aircraft, with the *yato* or squadron consisting of three flights of nine to twelve aircraft. An *orlyak* (wing) was formed of three *yato*, plus a staff flight, giving a total strength of around 40 aircraft. Top of the hierarchy was the *polk* (regiment), comprising 120 aircraft of a single type such as fighters or bombers. Five air regiments were formed, as follows.

The First Army Reconnaissance *Polk* comprised three reconnaissance *orlyak* and one separate *yato*, as well as a seaplane *orlyak* assigned directly to the field army. The air *eskadra,* under independent command, was formed by the 2nd Storm *Polk*, the 5th Bomber *Polk* and the 6th Fighter *Polk*. The last regiment to be formed was the Air Training *Polk*. Two numbers separated by a full point designated each *Orlyak*, so that 2 .6, for example, was the designation of the 2nd *Orlyak* of the 6th *Polk*.

Obsolete Czech-built B 534 fighters formed the backbone of the *Vazdushni Vojski* (Royal Bulgarian Air Force) fighter arm prior to the Bf 109 entering service

Groundcrews rush to their B 534s during a practice scramble at Vrazhdebna airfield in the summer of 1941

In January 1941 Bulgarian fighter units were equipped with 73 B 534s, 18 Bf 109E-3s and E-4s and 11 P.24Bs.

UNDER ATTACK

Even before the German attack, Yugoslav aircraft had conducted reconnaissance flights over Bulgaria, but this changed dramatically at 0845 hrs on 6 June when Yugoslav Do 17s dropped the first bombs to fall on Bulgarian territory in World War 2. Their target was Kyustendil, a small town 12 miles (20 km) from the Yugoslav border. This was followed by limited bombardments of Petrich, Ihtiman and Varba airfields (where Luftwaffe units were based), Sofia railway station and other smaller towns and villages. Later, it emerged that most of the attacks were conducted by RAF Wellingtons based in Greece. Although their effect was mostly psychological, since little damage was done, they did demonstrate the complete inefficiency of Bulgarian air defences. The raids ceased with the Greek capitulation on 23 June 1941.

Although defence against these attacks was mainly by anti-aircraft artillery, there were some attempts made to intercept the bombers with B 534 fighters (known as *Dogan* – hunting falcon) from 6.2 *Orlyak*, based at Bozhurishte. Podporuchik Petar Petrov recalled;

'In the first days of the conflict our wing, led by podporuchik Dimitar Spisarevski, scrambled to intercept a lone Yugoslav Do 17 on its way to Sofia. However, the bomber turned south and we could not catch it. Later, we heard that it surprised German units based at Varba airfield.'

The real air war over Bulgaria, however, erupted with the beginning of Operation *Tidal Wave*, which saw the Allies target the Ploesti oilfields in Rumania. Nine day and eight night raids were made involving a total of 2000 aircraft. Karlovo airfield was bombed twice and 80 Bulgarian aircraft were destroyed on the ground. Then, at 0800 hrs on Sunday,

The B 534 was not an easy aircraft to land thanks to its narrow-track, fixed undercarriage. This scene was often repeated at various grass airfields across Bulgaria. Here, *podporuchik* Gerov has stood his fighter on its nose at the end of a training flight in the autumn of 1942

Pilots of 2.6 *Orlyak* discuss their last flight in front of a recently-arrived D.520 at Karlovo airfield in the early autumn of 1943

1 August 1943, 177 USAAF B-24 Liberators left their base near Benghazi, in Libya, on yet another raid on Ploesti. The formation was spotted during its flight over the Mediterranean, and at 1215 hrs Bulgarian fighter units at Bozhurishte, Vrazhdebna and Karlovo airfields were alerted.

Karlovo was the base of 3.6 *Orlyak*, which was equipped with the most advanced fighters available in Bulgaria at the time – Bf 109G-2s. The first batch of 23 brand-new aircraft had been delivered to the unit in March 1943. The first element to be scrambled was the duty flight of three aircraft, led by poruchik Mikhail Grigorov. Five minutes later the second flight departed under the command of poruchik Lyuben Kondakov. The last to go were the four aircraft of poruchik Stoyan Stoyanov. At the same time ten thoroughly obsolete B 534s were also patrolling over Sofia, although their attempts to meet the attackers met with complete failure.

Pavel Pavlov poses on the wing of his Bf 109E-4, which displays the emblem of the 672nd *Yato*, 3.6 fighter *Orlyak* (inspired by the *Gruppe* emblem of IV./JG 1). The marking was applied by fellow *Emil* pilot Mikhail Grigorov

Poruchik Stoyan Stoyanov poses on the cockpit sill of his Bf 109G-2 soon after scoring his first aerial victories on 1 August 1943, when he shot down two USAAF B-24 Liberators

After a lengthy, but fruitless, patrol over Sofia, Stoyanov decided to land at Vrazhdebna.

At around 1500 hrs the fighters took off again to meet the bombers on their return from Ploesti. This time the intercepting force was comprised of just four Bf 109Gs, for Vrazhdebna lacked maintenance facilities for the rapid servicing of advanced aircraft, delaying the scrambling of Stoyanov's wing. In the meantime, B 534s had encountered 18 bombers near Vratsa, but their attack was inconclusive. The Bulgarian pilots opened fire at too great a range, and although they continued shooting until they passed through the formation, their 7.92 mm machine guns were ineffective against the heavily armoured American bombers.

The Bulgarian pilots immediately initiated a second attack, but they could only catch up with the bombers near the border town of Kyustendil after a pursuit of over 90 miles (150 km). The result of the second attack was exactly the same as the first.

A few minutes after the *Dogans'* first attack, the four Bf 109s encountered the bombers. Stoyanov, later to become the top-scoring Bulgarian ace, recalled;

'I approached the rear of the column, flying at the same level following the prevailing tactical doctrine. My wingman, podporuchik Bonev,

Stoyan Stoyanov poses in front of a wing salvaged from the wreckage of one of the B-24s that he shot down on 1 August 1943

followed closely. We were flying at least 125 mph (200 kmh) faster than the bombers, and soon overtook them. After a few seconds we saw traces of enemy fire coming towards us. At first it seemed to be coming from a few turrets, but soon they all opened fire on us. I have never seen so much tracer passing so close. It was terrible, but I didn't have time to get scared. I escaped from the deadly fire and started thinking about how to continue the attack. I decided to go against the rules and make a frontal attack.

'Giving my aeroplane full throttle, I flew about six miles (10 km) ahead the bomber formation. I turned through 180 degrees and rushed at the four-engined bombers from the sun. I selected the leading bomber in the formation as my target.

'As I opened fire, I could see my shells and bullets shatter the glazed nose of the heavy machine. After a few seconds I had to change course to avoid ramming the bomber. At that moment it nosed down and I stitched its fuselage from nose to tail with my fire. It dived and disappeared from my view. I passed less than 20 ft (5 m) over the bombers, so they were not able to fire at me.'

This was the first aerial victory of the war for the Bulgarian fighter force. But Stoyanov had not finished. His second attack was also made against tactical rules. He approached one of the last bombers in the formation from behind and below. His fire caused the bomber's two left engines to gush heavy black smoke, and it too slowly dropped out of formation.

The heroes of the 1 August 1943 battle receive Bulgarian and German decorations. They are, from left to right, podporuchik Petar Bochev (five kills), kapitan Chudomir Toplodolski (four kills), poruchik Stoyan Stoyanov (five kills) and podporuchik Christo Krastev (one kill). This is one of the few existing photographs of Bulgaria's second highest scoring fighter pilot, Petar Bochev

Podporuchik Petar Bochev copied Stoyanov, but he flew so close to his target that he almost rammed it. He opened fire from 160 ft (50 m), and the bomber exploded – only the tail gunner escaped. Bochev's aircraft was heavily damaged by both defensive fire and the explosion, but the man who was to become the second highest scoring Bulgarian ace still made it back to base. However, his element leader, podoruchik Christo Krastev, force-landed near Ferdinand out of fuel.

It had been a successful day for the Bulgarian fighter pilots, Stoyanov's wing shooting down a total of five heavy bombers. In addition to the two credited to Stoyanov himself, Bochev, Krastev and podporuchik Bonev had each shot down a B-24.

BOMBING OFFENSIVE

Despite its ferocity, the air battle had not resulted from any deliberate intention by the Allies to target Bulgaria. That was about to change. At the Casablanca Conference held in January 1943, Allied chiefs of staff initiated a combined strategic bombing offensive against Germany. Its primary purpose was to sap the Reich's ability to prosecute the war, but a subsidiary objective was to separate Bulgaria from the Axis through a sustained campaign of day and night bombing. This task was allocated in October to the Mediterranean Allied Strategic Air Force, under Gen Ira Eaker. The US Fifteenth Air Force, based at Foggia, Italy, became operational on 1 November 1943 to provide the day bomber force and the RAF's No 205 Group conducted night bombing. Inevitably, the main target was Sofia, and ten large-scale raids were launched against it between 14 November 1943 and 17 April 1944.

Meanwhile, Bulgaria was considering the implications of 1 August 1943. But first there were heroes to acclaim. Both Stoyan Stoyanov and Petar Bochev were decorated personally by the tsar with the Bravery Cross. Of the B-534 pilots, podporuchiks Vaptsarov and Daskalov were the only ones to get close enough to the bombers to attack, and they were also decorated. Clearly, though, the events of 1 August had shown that the B 534 could no longer be regarded as a credible interceptor.

Pilots of 3.6 *Orlyak* gather for a photograph in January 1944 at Bozhurishte. They are, from left to right, Ivan Bonev (four kills), Dimitar Vujchev, Stoyan Stoyanov (five kills), Joto Kamenov and Ivan Demirev

**Poruchik Petar Manolev of 3.6
Orlyak poses in front of his Bf 109G
at Bozhurishte in June 1944**

Stoyanov's extemporised tactics resulted in the development of new ways for fighters to attack heavy bombers, as fellow Bf 109 pilot poruchik (now polkovnik) Petar Manolev recalled;

'We were extensively trained to attack heavy bombers using a manoeuvre we had developed. At first it was thought that the fighter should climb and attack the bomber from above and behind, which meant a steep dive from the rear at 10 or 15 degrees ether side of the bomber's course. Now, about 500 m (1500 ft) below the bomber, we had to climb at top speed straight up, which allowed us to fire a two- or three-second burst from below, where the bombers were less well protected.'

Many of the subsequent victories by Bulgarian pilots were achieved after such manoeuvres had been flown. Similar tactics were employed by Luftwaffe ace Adolf Galland and his pilots as they battled against Allied heavy bombers over Germany.

On 12 August 3.6 *Orlyak*, with its 16 Bf 109G-2s, was deployed to Bozhurishte to defend Sofia against air attack. The city's ground-based defences were also considerably strengthened over the coming months. But decorating the heroes of 1 August was one of the last public acts to be performed by the king. On 28 August Boris III died suddenly. The reason for his death is unknown, but there are suspicions that he was assassinated. Whatever the cause, his death was a blow to the air force because he was its

Equipped with an external belly tank, a Bf 109G-2 of 3.6 *Orlyak* sits in the snow at Vrazhdebna airfield in January 1944

chief patron. It also added a degree of instability, since his son Simeon was under age, so a regency council was appointed.

THE FIRST RAID

The first raid on Sofia came on 14 November 1943 when about 90 B-25 medium bombers, escorted by 100 P-38s, approached the city just after noon in two waves, flying at about 16,000 ft. The defences were alerted late, and the first of the 3.6 *Orlyak* Bf 109s was scrambled just as the B-25s were about to release their bombs. However, 13 Messerschmitts engaged the escort and one P-38 was confirmed as shot down for the loss of one of the defending fighters, and its pilot, plus two others damaged.

The USAAF mounted its second raid nine days later, and again 13 Bf 109s were waiting for the attacking B-24s. A combination of fighter attacks, stiff anti-aircraft defences and broken cloud over the target area meant that only 17 of the bombers were able to drop their bombs on their assigned targets. The fighters continued to press home their attacks, scoring several confirmed and probable kills. The wrecks of only two B-24s were subsequently found, despite the BBC in London reporting that the losses had amounted to ten bombers. The defenders lost one pilot and three aircraft, with three more Bf 109s extensively damaged.

The third raid on 10 December involved 50 B-24s, escorted by about 60 P-38s. As well as meeting the Bf 109s of 3.6 *Orlyak* again, they encountered the Dewoitine D.520s of Vrazhdebna-based 2.6 *Orlyak* for the first time. The escorting fighters, more numerous than in the two previous raids, were more successful and no kills were confirmed. The defenders lost one D.520 and its pilot. The Bulgarian were, however, able to reduce the effectiveness of what might otherwise have been a damaging raid. As it was, 100 buildings were destroyed but only 30 casualties were reported.

Ten days later the attackers were back with 50 B-24s Liberators and a similar number of P-38s. Over Yugoslavia, the formation split into two waves and the larger group turned north, convincing *Vazdushni Vojski* command that they were making for Ploesti. To meet the southern group, 16 Bf 109Gs and 24 D.520s were scrambled at 1230 hrs. Battle

was joined over the village Dolni Pasarel, near Sofia, and between the Vitosha and Lozenska mountains.

RAMMING ATTACK!

Poruchik Dimitar Spisarevski was a member of the 3.6 *Orlyak* staff flight, and there are many accounts in the reports and memoirs of surviving pilots of both sides of his extraordinary part in this battle. His first attack against a Liberator lagging a little behind the main formation was not successful. He opened fire from too great a range, but despite heavy defensive fire he tried again. Quickly closing on another four-engined bomber, Spisarevski was able to score his first kill, but moments later he made the last attack of his life.

3.6 *Orlyak* staff flight pilot Dimitar Spisarevski (seated, second from left) attempts to keep warm with pilots of his *Yato* at Vrazhdebna airfield in late 1943

A hastily camouflaged Bf 109G-6 of 3.6 *Orlyak* sits out in the open at an unidentified airfield in August 1944

'Poruchik Spisarevski shot down an enemy Liberator bomber which crashed in pieces to the ground', is the matter-of-fact language used by the 3.6 *Orlyak* combat diary to describe what happened next. It continued;

'This was his first combat. Being engrossed in his task of shooting down as many bombers as possible, poruchik Spisarevski rammed one of the enemy bombers at full speed. Both machines crashed. So died one of the best pilots, and a brave soldier.'

Understandably, more emotive language was used by 24-year-old Sgt Robert Henry Rener, a gunner on board the Liberator rammed by Spisarevski. The only member of its crew to survive, he was captured soon after the battle and spent several days in a hospital. During his subsequent interrogation, Rener stated;

'It was a real hell. Three minutes into the battle we were shocked to see one of our bombers go down in flames. Only a minute later our aircraft was shaken by a terrible hit. I saw the engines catch fire and I don't know what exactly happened to me after that. I felt a blow on the head and passed out. I was probably thrown out of the aeroplane still holding my machine gun. The parachute opened automatically, and I must have dropped the gun. I came to on the ground. The attack by your fighters was terrible. I will never forget it.'

The same event was described also by 23-year-old 2Lt John McLendon, a P-38 Lightning pilot with the USAAF's 97th FS/82nd FG who was also shot down, probably by *poruchik* Nikolaj Jordanov. An eyewitness to both of Spisarevski's successes, he reported;

'About six minutes before I crashed with my fighter I saw something incredible, and I don't know if any other American pilots have seen anything like it over Europe. I saw a Bulgarian fighter shoot down one bomber then immediately attack another. With all guns firing, the fighter rammed the bomber's belly and cut off its tail. It was flown by one of our best crews. It was a really terrible death even for the bravest pilot.'

According to the official list of Bulgarian fighter pilots' victories, Spisarevski was credited with only one victory, despite the large number of eyewitnesses confirming his second. The reason for this error remains unclear, and no other Bulgarian pilot was credited with shooting down the Liberator, which crashed near Pasarel.

Meanwhile, the northern group of American bombers was not heading for Ploesti. Its ruse had been successful, and it was able to reach Sofia and drop 270 bombs, including 67 500-kg weapons, on the capital. But the attackers paid dearly for their success. The Americans were pursued by fighters until they left Bulgarian airspace, with the result that three B-24s and seven P-38s – ten per cent of the attacking force – were shot down, with five more damaged. Podporuchik Gencho Dimitrov was credited with a B-24 shot down near Pasarel. Two Bf 109s were lost, however. Podporuchik Georgi Kyumyurdjiev was killed soon after he had accounted for a P-38. Mikhail Banov survived a crash-landing, and two other machines were damaged, although they returned safely to base.

A UNIQUE VICTORY

The Czech-designed B 135B formed the main equipment of the Bulgarian fighter pilots' school at Dolna Mitropoliya. Twelve were imported as kits in 1943, but immediately after their assembly at Lovetch and the type's first

Kapitan Krastyo Atanasov is seen in the cockpit of Avia B 135 'White 3' at Dolna Mitropoliya in 1944. He was flying this machine on 30 March 1944 when he shared in the destruction of a B-24 with fellow fighter pilots' school instructor feldfebel Jordan Ferdinandov

test flights, it became clear that the aircraft was both underpowered undergunned – it boasted just two 7.92 mm machine guns, the intended engine-mounted 20 mm canon having been deleted. This meant that the aircraft was fit only to serve as an advanced trainer.

When the Allied raids began, four of the aircraft were detached and maintained as an alert force to defend the airfield and nearby towns. Its primary aim, however, was to provide pupils with the opportunity to gain experience. They were certainly to receive it on 30 March 1944. At 0930 hrs, a large formation comprising over 450 B-24s and B-17s, escorted by about 150 P-38s and, for the first time over Bulgaria, P-51 Mustangs, was detected over Scopie, heading for Sofia. This was one of the largest forces to threaten the country so far, and all available fighters were altered.

The fighter school's CO, kapitan Krastyo Atanasov, ordered the alert force to scramble. Soon, four B 135Bs ('White 3', '4', '5' and '11') were airborne and heading for Sofia. At their controls were Atanasov and instructors feldfebel Jordan Ferdinandov, podporuchik Petar Manolev and feldfebel Nedyo Kolev. Atanasov recalled;

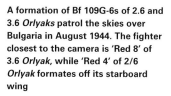

A formation of Bf 109G-6s of 2.6 and 3.6 *Orlyaks* patrol the skies over Bulgaria in August 1944. The fighter closest to the camera is 'Red 8' of 3.6 *Orlyak*, while 'Red 4' of 2/6 *Orlyak* formates off its starboard wing

Three Bf 109G-6s of 3.6 *Orlyak* go in search of USAAF bombers in late July 1944. The aircraft in the foreground is 'Green 1', flown by the squadron CO poruchik Petar Manolev, and previously by poruchik Stoyan Stoyanov. The aircraft behind it is 'Green 7', flown by podporuchik Evgeni Tonchev. This photograph was taken from 'Green 6 ' by podporuchik Pavel Pavlov

Ivan Petrov of 3.6 *Orlyak*. Although Petrov is not among the most prominent of Bulgarian fighter pilots, his aircraft displays an interesting personal emblem

'We sighted the fourth wave of American bombers heading for Sofia over Vratsa and Ferdinand. Later, we saw fighters from 3.6 and 2.6 *Orlyaks* land at Bozhurishte and Vrazhdebna airfields to refuel and rearm after the combat, and it was obvious that after three waves of bombers no one expected a fourth. So to our great surprise it was just the four of us against 60 or 70 American bombers in the sky over Sofia! Below us, the city was in flames, but I was encouraged because this bomber group was flying without fighter escort. We attacked several times without success. But somewhere over Radomir, when the Americans had released their bombs and were hurrying south-west to their bases, their formations broke up.

'We attacked a bomber which had dropped behind the others a little. I concentrated my fire on one of the engines and set it on fire. My wingman, feldfebel Ferdinandov, did the same to the next engine. The heavy machine started to lose height towards the mountains. With the last droplets of fuel in our tanks, we landed at Bozhurishte airfield, where we immediately reported what had happened.'

Atanasov and Ferdinandov were credited with a shared victory in the wake of what would prove to be the only combat mission ever performed by the B 135. But fellow instructor Petar Manolev had a different recollection of the combat;

'The effect of our fire against the target was insignificant. The speed of our fighters was almost equal to that of the bombers. We couldn't even think of repeating the attack. Pursuing the enemy to the south-west towards Pernik, we were fired at by our own anti-aircraft artillery and we had to manoeuvre to escape it. Meanwhile, the leading pair (Atanasov and Ferdinandov) continued after the enemy aeroplanes. I estimated that we were very close to the operating range of the aircraft, so I decided to return to Dolna Mitropoliya, where we landed at 1130 hrs on the last drops of fuel. A little later the other pair landed at Bozhurishte, home base of 3.6 *Orlyak*. There, Krastyo Atanasov reported that they had shot down a bomber. My personal opinion of the mission is that the pilots fired all their ammunition but did not shoot down a bomber.'

In his report, Ferdinandov stated that he had seen five men bale out of the Liberator that he and Atsanov had attacked, and that the bomber had crashed near Tran soon afterwards. According to Atanasov, the school's instructors had made several further attempts to intercept enemy bombers while flying the B 135, but had not been able to make contact with them.

That same day 3.6 *Orlyak* was ordered to intercept the bombers before they reached Sofia. They were encountered flying in tight formation at an altitude of 20,000 ft, with their P-38 escort above them at about 25,000-27,000 ft. Podporuchik Christo Kostakiev charged the bombers at full throttle and fired at one from no more than 150 ft. His burst was aimed at the Liberator's bomb-bay, and there was a huge explosion. In fact it was so great that it destroyed the next aircraft in the formation. Only the two pilots of the second B-24 were able to escape by parachute.

Kostakiev's Bf 109G-6 was also badly damaged. He recalled;

'I had no time to think about my victory. My aeroplane was trailing white vapour and there were big holes in the wings. I assumed that the radiator was hit so I had to switch the engine off.'

Kostakiev faced two choices – glide down to a belly-landing or take to his parachute. He chose the former, and from 2000 ft he saw a field below which appeared suitable. As he got closer, he discovered that it was anything but. Kostakiev survived the resulting crash without injury. This was his first combat mission.

Podporuchik **Christo Kostakiev is seen soon after the mission in which he shot down two B-24s with a single well-aimed burst of cannon fire**

This Bf 109G was written when its pilot was forced to crash-land after suffering battle damage

These Dewoitine D.520s, still displaying German insignia, were photographed shortly after their arrival in Bulgaria in late 1943

D.520s sit side-by-side at Karlovo airfield in the early spring of 1944 Despite the poor quality of this photograph, a Luftwaffe-style chevron is visible on the fuselage immediately below the cockpit of the aircraft on the left

Sofia endured its final air raid on 17 March – a black day in Bulgarian aviation history. This time 350 B-24s were escorted by 100 fighters, but not the familiar twin-boom P-38s. Instead, the Bulgarian fighter pilots were about to encounter the P-47 Thunderbolt and the formidable P-51 Mustang. The defenders – just 30 Bf-109Gs and seven D.520s – were able to account for two B-24s and two P-51s. For the second time one of the bombers was downed in a ramming attack, but unlike Dimitar Spisarevski, poruchik Nedelcho Bonchev survived by taking to his parachute. Anti-aircraft artillery fired over 3000 rounds and hit eight more bombers, some of which failed to return to their bases,

But the Bulgarians paid a heavy price, losing nine of the defending fighters and having six pilots killed. Among the victims were poruchik Lyuben Kondakov, podporuchik Ivan Stefanov and poruchik Veselin Rachev. The CO of 2.6 *Orlyak,* kapitan Nikolaj Boshnyakov, had a lucky

A training alert scramble for 2.6 *Orlyak* has pilots and groundcrews scrambling for their D.520s at Karlovo at the end of January 1944

Some 96 ex-Vichy French and newly-manufactured D.520s were supplied to Bulgaria from German stocks during the course of 1943. The bulk of these machines were issued to 2.6 *Orlyak* at Karlovo

escape. His aircraft was hit and he baled out, but did not disconnect his radio cable quickly enough and he remained attached to the aircraft from it as the fighter plunged earthward from a height of 20,000 ft. Boshnyakov passed out and eventually the cable snapped, allowing him to recover consciousness and deploy his parachute just before he hit the ground. He duly recovered after a long stay in a hospital.

The final raid of the Allied aerial campaign against Bulgaria came on 26 August 1944, and two American heavy bombers were shot down. Since Bulgaria had joined the Axis, it had detected over 23,000 incursions by enemy aircraft into its airspace. In reply, defending fighters had sortied a total of 1100 times, Bulgarian fighter pilots participating in more than 760 aerial combats in which 56 enemy aircraft had been shot down. Bulgarian losses totalled 27 aircraft and 23 pilots killed. Some 1828 civilians had been killed and 2372 injured during the Allied bombing raids.

On 9 September the Patriotic Front (which included communists) seized power in Bulgaria. The Soviet army crossed the border and the

Bf 109G-6/trop 'White 7', with its distinctive Erla hood, was part of the last batch of Messerschmitt fighters delivered to Bulgaria in the summer of 1944. It is seen here on patrol with poruchik Somov of 3.6 *Orlyak* at the controls

country left the Axis and almost immediately declared war on its former ally. As a result of the change of sides, the *Vaqzdushni Vojski* was engaged in operations over Yugoslavia. The main task for the fighter regiments was the close support of the army, with occasional escort missions for ground attack units. But the intensity of aerial combats during what came to be known as the Patriotic War was at a lower level than before.

Bulgaria's leading ace, Stoyan Stoyanov, survived both the war and the change of political control. In fact, he rose to the rank of major general and commanded the fighter arm along the way. On 9 September 1947 Maj Stoyanov led a formation 25 Yak-9s in a flypast over Sofia to celebrate the third anniversary of the *coup* which had brought the communists to power in Bulgaria.

Petar Bochev, Bulgaria's second-highest scorer of the war, remains the unknown ace. There is hardly any mention of him in historical literature, nor in his contemporaries' memoirs. According to Stoyanov, Bochev was killed on 5 October 1944 during an attack on German artillery in support of Bulgarian infantry in Yugoslavia. The belly tank of his aircraft was hit and caught fire, and as he was too low to escape by parachute, he decided to make a belly-landing. Stoyanov was an eyewitness to the whole event, and according to his account, Bochev was the second to attack. His leader, kapitan Atanasov, had taken the Germans by surprise, while Stoyanov was behind Bochev, preparing to attack. He later recalled;

'Suddenly I saw flames underneath his aircraft. Then it disappeared, but after a moment it burned intensely and flames shot out about 10 m (30 ft) behind him. He turned away and headed towards flatter ground, gliding in for a belly landing. I abandoned my attack and flew just above him. His aircraft touched down but exploded before it had stopped. I almost lost control of my aircraft. The space in the formation between myself and kapitan Atanasov remained empty. After that it was just like a bad dream.'

APPENDICES

Comparative Ranks

Slovak	Bulgarian	Luftwaffe	English translation
-	general	general der Flieger	-
general I. triedy	general-leytenant	generalleutnant	general
general II. triedy	general-major	generalmajor	lieutenant general
plukovnik	polkovnik	oberst	colonel
podplukovnik	podpolkovnik	oberstleutnant	lieutenant colonel
major	major	major	major
stotnik	kapitan	hauptmann	captain
nadporucik	porucik	oberleutnant	first lieutenant
porucik	podporucik	leutnant	second lieutenant
	feldfebel	stabsfeldwebel	-
zastupca dostojnicky	-	oberfeldwebel	warrant officer
zastavnik	-	feldwebel	master sergeant
rotnik	podofitiser	unterfeldwebel	staff sergeant
catnik	kandidat podofitiser	unteroffizier	sergeant
desiatnik	-	obergefreiter	corporal
slobodnik	efreitor	Gefreiter	lance corporal
strelnik	rednik	flieger	Private

Slovak Aces

	Confirmed claims in campaigns					
Rank and Name	Poland 1939	USSR 1941-43	Home Defence 1944	Uprising 1944	Total	Notes
M/Sgt Jan Reznak	-	32	-	-	32	
M/Sgt Izidor Kovarik	-	28	-	-	28	KIFA 11/7/44
1Lt Jan Gerthofer	-	26	-	-	26	PoW 31/8/44
M/Sgt Frantisek Cyprich	-	12	-	2 +1 shared	14 + 1 shared	
M/Sgt Frantisek Brezina	-	14	-	-	14	
M/Sgt Pavol Zelenak	-	12	-	-	12	WIA 26/6/44
M/Sgt Jozef Stauder	-	12	-	-	12	
S/Sgt Anton Matusek	-	12	-	-	12	Desertion 9/9/43
S/Sgt Rudolf Bozik	-	8	1	2 + 1 shared	11 + 1 shared	WIA 26/9/43
Sgt Alexander Geric	-	9	-	-	9	Desertion 11/9/43
1Lt Vladimir Krisko	-	9	-	-	9	
Sgt Jozef Jancovic	-	7	-	-	7	KIA 30/3/43
Sgt Rudolf Palaticky	-	6	-	-	6	WIA 18/7/43
S/Sgt Frantisek Hanovec	0 +1 shared	5	-	-	5 + 1	PoW 17/11/44
1Lt Juraj Puskar	-	5	-	-	5	KIA 26/6/44
S/Sgt Stefan Ocvirk	-	5	-	-	5	
S/Sgt Stefan Martis	-	5	-	-	5	

Slovakian Aces' Claims

JAN REZNAK

Date	Time	Claim	Location
17/1/43	0635	I-153	W of Smolenskaya
28/1/43	1110	I-16	SW of Akhtyrskaya
11/2/43	0742	I-153	S of Krymskaya
10/3/43	0952	I-16	S of Akhtyrskaya
11/3/43	0750	I-153	S of Abinskaya
11/3/43	0754	I-16	W of Yerivanskaya
13/3/43	0725	LaGG-3	NE of Petrovskaya
14/3/43	1457	DB-3	Krasnoarmeyskaya
27/3/43	0935	LaGG-3	SW of Petrovskaya
29/3/43	0937	DB-3	SE of Slavyanskaya
29/3/43	0942	I-153	Petrovskaya
31/3/43	0646	LaGG-3	SE of Petrovskaya
10/4/43	0636	LaGG-3	ESE of Slavyanskaya
15/4/43	1153	LaGG-3	N of Gelendzik
20/4/43	0559	LaGG-3	S of Slavyanskaya
20/4/43	0630	LaGG-3	W of Slavyanskaya
21/4/43	1355	LaGG-3	Akhtyrskaya
25/4/43	1622	LaGG-3	S of Gelendzik
27/4/43	1746	LaGG-3	Kholmskaya
27/4/43	1748	LaGG-3	Kholmskaya
27/4/43	1815	I-16	SW of Abinskaya
30/4/43	1217	LaGG-3	E of Krymskaya
3/5/43	1255	LaGG-3	S of Krymskaya
3/5/43	1506	I-16	SW of Krymskaya
3/5/43	1512	LaGG-3	S of Krymskaya
4/5/43	0650	MiG-3	NW of Gelendzik
10/5/43	0855	MiG-3	Kholmskaya
26/5/43	1245	LaGG-3	W of Krymskaya
26/5/43	1810	Pe-2	S of Troyickaya
29/5/43	0847	MiG-3	SE of Troyickaya
20/6/43	1647	Yak-1	SE of Abinskaya
30/6/43	0803	LaGG-3	N of Slavyanskaya

IZIDOR KOVARIK

Date	Time	Claim	Location
28/1/43	0845	I-16	S of Shapsugskaya
11/2/43	0740	I-16	NW of Shapsugskaya
25/2/43	1356	Il-2	Sea of Azov, N of Temryuk
10/3/43	0953	I-16	SE of Akhtyrskaya
11/3/43	0751	I-153	SE of Yerivanskaya
11/3/43	0752	I-153	ESE of Yerivanskaya
12/3/43	0842	Il-2	S of Sennaya
13/3/43	0727	LaGG-3	NE of Petrovskaya
17/3/43	0827	I-16	SE of Starodzereliyevskaya
22/3/43	1434	I-16	SE of Slavyanskaya
22/3/43	1436	I-16	SE of Slavyanskaya
29/3/43	0937	DB-3	E of Troyickaya
29/3/43	0941	LaGG-3	W of Krasnoarmeyskaya
31/3/43	0645	LaGG-3	SE of Petrovskaya
10/4/43	0635	LaGG-3	E of Slavyanskaya
15/4/43	1152	LaGG-3	E of Yerivanskaya
15/4/43	1155	LaGG-3	E of Yerivanskaya
20/4/43	0558	LaGG-3	S of Slavyanskaya
21/4/43	1355	LaGG-3	?
25/4/43	1620	LaGG-3	S of Gelendzik
27/4/43	1744	Boston	N of Achtyrskaya
27/4/43	1813	MiG-3	?
26/5/43	1511	Yak-1	N of Krymskaya
29/5/43	0845	Yak-1	NE of Troyickaya
29/5/43	0853	Yak-1	SW of Troyickaya
29/5/43	1210	Yak-1	SW of Troyickaya
29/5/43	1215	Yak-1	W of Troyickaya
17/6/43	0515	Yak-1	NW of Krasnoarmeyskaya

JAN GERTHOFER

Date	Time	Claim	Location
29/12/42	1218	I-16	N of Tuapse
17/1/43	1345	LaGG-3	SW of Smolenskaya
12/3/43	0615	I-16	SW of Grivenskaya
14/3/43	0510	LaGG-3	Sea of Azov, N of Akhtanizovskaya
15/3/43	0751	Il-2	Sea of Azov, W of Petrovskaya
15/3/43	0753	Il-2	Sea of Azov, N of Temrjuk
21/3/43	1128	Pe-2	Black Sea, SE of Myschako
30/3/43	0603	I-16	W of Petrovskaya
30/3/43	1305	I-16	N of Anastasijevskaya
16/4/43	1203	LaGG-3	Black Sea, S of Gelendzik
16/4/43	1205	Airacobra	Black Sea, S of Gelendzik
19/4/43	1652	LaGG-3	Black Sea, S of Anapa
21/4/43	0926	Il-2	Black Sea, SSW of Anapa
21/4/43	1135	Airacobra	?
24/4/43	0831	Il-2	SE of Grivenskaya
24/4/43	0835	LaGG-3	NW of Kalininskaya
24/4/43	1648	LaGG-3	Solncedar
24/4/43	1650	Boston	E of Novorossiysk
30/4/43	1216	LaGG-3	NE of Novorossiysk
3/5/43	1505	Il-2	SW of Krymskaya
3/5/43	1510	LaGG-3	S of Krymskaya
26/5/43	1509	Yak-1	S of Svistelnikov
28/5/43	0710	La-5	S of Troyickaya
28/5/43	1042	Yak-1	Varenikovskaya
28/5/43	1052	Yak-1	W of Troyickaya
14/6/43	0630	Yak-1	WSW of Petrovskaya

FRANTISEK CYPRICH

Date	Time	Claim	Location
31/1/43	1130	Il-2	Kropotkin
10/2/43	1010	I-153	SW of Neberdzajevskaya
26/3/43	1127	Il-2	E of Yerivanskaya
29/3/43	1654	LaGG-3	W of Petrovskaya
19/4/43	1653	LaGG-3	Black Sea, SW of Anapa
27/4/43	1620	La-5	Krymskaya
30/4/43	1625	LaGG-3	SE of Krymskaya
4/5/43	0902	LaGG-3	S of Krymskaya
4/5/43	0910	LaGG-3	NW of Gelendzik
20/6/43	1645	Yak-1	SE of Abinskaya
20/6/43	1654	Yak-1	SE of Abinskaya
30/6/43	0802	LaGG-3	N of Slavyanskaya
2/9/44	0930	Ju 52/3m	Radvan
6/9/44	1810	Fw 189*	Kremnicka
12/9/44	0830	Ju 88	N of Brezno nr Hronom

* shared with Bozik

FRANTISEK BREZINA

Date	Time	Claim	Location
12/12/42	1347	MiG- 3	Tuapse
11/1/43	0635	I-153	N of Defanovka
16/1/43	0808	I-16	Black Sea, S of Gelendzik
2/2/43	1115	I-16	SW of Smolenskaya
15/3/43	0750	Il-2	Sea of Azov, W of Petrovskaya
15/3/43	0754	Il-2	Sea of Azov, N of Temryuk
20/3/43	1355	Boston	Black Sea, S of Myschako
30/3/43	0604	I-16	W of Petrovskaya
13/5/43	1040	Yak-1	NW of Troyickaya
26/5/43	1513	Yak-1	N of Krymskaya
28/5/43	0655	Yak-1	W of Troyickaya
28/5/43	0700	Yak-1	S of Troyickaya
28/5/43	1059	Yak-1	E of Varenikovskaya
14/6/43	0640	Il-2	SW of Petrovskaya

PAVEL ZELENAK

Date	Time	Claim	Location
28/1/43	0617	I-153	SE of Yerivanskaya
9/2/43	1040	Il-2	Troyickaya
16/3/43	0535	Il-2	Sea of Azov, SW of Acuyevo
16/3/43	0540	I-16	Sea of Azov, SW of Acuyevo
16/4/43	1206	LaGG-3	Katchalinskaya
20/4/43	0640	Il-2	SE of Slavyanskaya
24/4/43	0830	Il-2	SE of Grivenskaya
24/4/43	0837	LaGG-3	NW of Kalininskaya
26/5/43	1805	LaGG-3	N of Krymskaya
28/5/43	0658	Yak-1	N of Krymskaya
30/5/43	0625	Yak-1	SE of Troyickaya
30/5/43	0630	Yak-1	Gostagayevskaya

JOZEF STAUDER

Date	Time	Claim	Location
13/1/43	1005	I-153	SW of Krymskaya
12/3/43	0620	I-16	SW of Grivenskaya
14/3/43	0507	LaGG-3	Sea of Azov, N of Temryuk
16/3/43	0537	Il-2	Sea of Azov, SW of Acuyevo
17/3/43	0826	I 16	SE of Starodzereliyevskaya
21/3/43	1445	I-16	Krasnoarmeyskaya
20/4/43	0638	Il-2	S of Slavyanskaya
30/4/43	0745	Il-2	Black Sea, S of Gelendzik
30/4/43	0755	LaGG-3	W of Abinskaya
28/5/43	0705	La-5	S of Troyickaya
29/5/43	1212	Yak-1	SW of Troyickaya
29/5/43	1217	Airacobra	S of Troyickaya

ANTON MATUSEK

Date	Time	Claim	Location
26/7/43	1100	Airacobra	E of Troyickaya
26/7/43	1103	Boston	E of Troyickaya
28/7/43	1430	Boston	Gelendzik
1/8/43	0950	La-5	Sea of Azov, N of Temrjuk
1/8/43	0951	Boston	Sea of Azov, N of Temrjuk
6/8/43	0935	LaGG-3	NW of Novovelitchkovskaya
12/8/43	1130	Boston	NW of Slavyanskaya
12/8/43	1132	Boston	SE of Petrovskaya
13/8/43	1040	Il-2	S of Svistelnikov
18/8/43	0815	Boston	SSE of Smolenskaya
18/8/43	0818	Spitfire	Black Sea, W of Gelendzik
21/8/43	1230	Airacobra	Abinskaya

RUDOLF BOZIK

Date	Time	Claim	Location
26/7/43	1055	R-5	E of Troyickaya
26/7/43	1059	Airacobra	E of Troyickaya
14/9/43	0638	Il-2	Black Sea, SW of Novorossiysk
18/9/43	626	Il-2	Varenikovskaya
20/9/43	0645	Il-2	Black Sea, S of Myschako
22/9/43	0645	LaGG-3	Kurtchanskaya
22/9/43	0720	Boston	Black Sea, SE of Feodosiya
26/9/43	0855	Il-2	N of Anapa
13/4/44	1230	Bf 110*	Podunajske Biskupice
6/9/44	1810	Fw 189**	Kremnicka
16/9/44	1550	Ju 88	Nova Bana
4/10/44	1050	Fw 189	S of Turciansky Sv/Martin

* claimed as Liberator
** shared with Cyprich

ALEXANDER GERIC

Date	Time	Claim	Location
28/7/43	1430	Boston	Gelendzik
28/7/43	1431	Boston	Gelendzik
6/8/43	0936	LaGG-3	NNW of Novovelitchkovskaya
7/8/43	1145	Il-2	N of Krymskaya
7/8/43	1755	Spitfire	Krymskaya
12/8/43	1133	Airacobra	NE of Petrovskaya
18/8/43	0814	Boston	Black Sea, SE of Myschako
18/8/43	0819	Boston	Black Sea, W of Gelendzik
5/9/43	0752	Il-2	Black Sea, SW of Anapa

VLADIMIR KRISKO

Date	Time	Claim	Location
28/7/43	1430	Boston	Gelendzik
28/7/43	1431	Boston	Gelendzik
6/8/43	0936	LaGG-3	NNW of Novovelitchkovskaya
7/8/43	1145	Il-2	N of Krymskaya
7/8/43	1755	Spitfire	Krymskaya
12/8/43	1133	Airacobra	NE of Petrovskaya
18/8/43	0814	Boston	Black Sea, SE of Myschako
18/8/43	0819	Boston	Black Sea, W of Gelendzik
5/9/43	0752	Il-2	Black Sea, SW of Anapa

JOZEF JANCOVIC

Date	Time	Claim	Location
29/12/42	1215	I-16	N of Tuapse
28/1/43	0620	I-153	S of Cholmskaja
3/2/43	0922	LaGG-3	W of Ponezhukay
17/3/43	0825	I-16	S of Grivenskaya
17/3/43	0828	I-16	NE of Petrovskaya
22/03/43	1433	I-153	NE of Troyickaya
22/03/43	1435	I-16	SE of Slavyanskaya

RUDOLF PALATICKY

Date	Time	Claim	Location
17/9/43	0825	Airacobra	S of Svistelnikov
24/9/43	0955	Il-2	Black Sea, S of Taman
24/9/43	1000	Il-2	Black Sea, S of Taman
26/9/43	0857	Il-2	N of Anapa
4/10/43	0830	Yak-1	Black Sea, S of Taman
16/10/43	0745	MiG-1	Kertsch Channel, S of Kertch

FRANTISEK HANOVEC

Date	Time	Claim	Location
6/9/39	1218	Lublin R-XIII*	Narsany, Slovakia
22/7/43	1145	Airacobra	N of Krymskaya
30/7/43	0958	Boston	SW of Primorsko-Achtarsk
26/9/43	1335	Yak-1	Black Sea, SW of Anapa
7/10/43	0755	Il-2	Sea of Azov, NW of Acujevo
27/10/43	1150	La-5	Kertch Channel, S of Kertch

* shared with Ziaran and Jaloviar

JURAJ PUSKAR

Date	Time	Claim	Location
30/7/43	0959	Airacobra	SW of Primorsko-Akhtarsk
30/7/43	1002	Airacobra	SW of Troyickaya
8/8/43	0930	Airacobra	W of Krymskaya
14/9/43	1645	Il-2	S of Svistelnikov
18/9/43	1625	Il-2	S of Svistelnikov

STEFAN OCVIRK

Date	Time	Claim	Location
7/9/43	0600	LaGG-3	S of Svistelnikov
4/10/43	1430	Boston	Sea of Azov, NE of Akhtanizovskaya
5/10/43	0525	Boston	Sea of Azov, NE of Akhtanizovskaya
6/10/43	1212	Yak-1	E of Starotitarevskaya
7/10/43	0910	LaGG-3	Kertch Channel, S of Kertch

STEFAN MARTIS

Date	Time	Claim	Location
30/07/43	1840	Il-2	SW of Troyickaya
12/08/43	0630	Il-2	S of Troyickaya
04/10/43	0825	Yak-1	Black Sea, S of Taman
05/10/43	0527	Yak-1	Sea of Azov, NE of Akhtanizovskaya
06/10/43	1210	Il-2	nr Starotitarevskaja

Tactical Markings of Bulgarian Fighters

In view of the close co-operation between Bulgarian and German fighter units in intercepting American and British aircraft, the *Vazdushni vojski* adopted the Luftwaffe's standard European theatre tactical markings of yellow wingtips and tail bands for its aircraft.

In September 1944, Bulgaria declared war on its former ally and participated in operations against the Germans in Yugoslavia alongside the Soviets, but after instances of misidentification of Bulgarian aircraft by Soviet pilots, the theatre tactical markings were changed from yellow to white. This remained in use until the end of the Bulgarian participation in the war in March 1945.

In addition, an identification code was used for every *yato* within a particular *orlyak*. The numbers of staff flight aircraft were painted in yellow, while those of the three *yatos* were applied in the colours of the Bulgarian national flag – white for the first *yato*, green for the second and red for the third. In some cases, such as with the D.520s of 2.6 *Orlyak*, propeller spinners were also painted to match the numbers.

With very few exceptions, fighters did not display personal markings, nor were aircraft assigned to a particular pilot. Typically, the machine carrying number 1 was flown by the *Yato* CO whenever possible, while the remaining pilots flew any aircraft that was ready for operational use.

Top-Scoring Bulgarian Fighter Pilots

When tallying the victories scored by its fighter pilots, the Bulgarian air force used a system similar to that employed by the Luftwaffe to assess pilots for promotion in units operating in the west. This system was confirmed by Secret Order No 19, issued by the CO of the *Vazdishni vojski* on 18 March 1944. This order also listed three possible results from combat with enemy aircraft:

1 – total destruction of aircraft flying in formation with others

2 – aircraft damaged badly enough to cause it to leave formation

3 – lone aircraft or one already damaged shot down.

Pilots achieving such results were credited with points according to the type of enemy aircraft involved, as follows:

Attacked aircraft	Points awarded by result		
	1	2	3
4-engined bomber in formation	3	2	1
4-engined bomber singly or damaged	-	-	1
2-engined bomber in formation	2	2	1
2-engined bomber singly or damaged	-	-	1
Fighter or other single-engined aircraft	1	1	1

Order No 78, dated 28 December 1944, gives the complete list of confirmed victories credited to Bulgarian fighter pilots in World War 2. Although issued by the Bulgarian Defence Ministry, some of the numbers in it are still disputed, and therefore regarded as doubtful.

The most successful Bulgarian fighter pilots listed appear in the table below. What is clear, however, is that only Stoyanov and Botchev fall within the accepted definition of an ace (i.e. five kills).

No	Rank, name, *yato* (*orlyak*)	Downed aircraft	Points awarded
1	*por* Stoyan Stoyanov, 682nd (3.6)	5 (+1*)	15
2	*podpor* Petar Botchev (3.6)	5	13
3	*kap* Tchudomir Toplodolski (CO 3.6)	4	8
4	*podpor* Ivan Bonev, 682nd (3.6)	4	8
5	*podpor* Gencho Ivanov, 692nd (3.6)	3	7
6	*podpor* Marin Tsvetkov, 672nd (3.6)	2	10
7	*por* Nedelcho Bonchev, CO 652nd (2.6)	2	8
8	*podpor* Petar Petrov (1.6)	2	8
9	*podpor* Christo Kostakiev (3.6)	2	6
10	*por* Dimitar Spisarevski (3.6) (2**)	3	(6**)
11	*kap* Krastyo Atanasov, CO Fighter School (3.6)	2	5
12	*feld* Christo Koev, 682nd (3.6)	2	4
13	*por* Vassil Shishkov (1.6)	2	2

* Includes one bomber shot down and one damaged (excluded from formation), instead of two bombers shot down
** Includes second B-24 Liberator destroyed in ramming attack and confirmed by captured American pilots but excluded from official list

1

B 534 (M-4) of catnik Jozef Stauder, No 13 Sqn (letka), Tulczyn, Ukraine, summer 1941

Up until 1942, these pre-war fighter biplanes were standard equipment for Slovakian fighter units. This particular aircraft displays the Slovakian Air Arms (Slovenske vzdusne zbrane, SVZ) camouflage scheme, with the wing uppersurfaces and fuselage sides in khaki overall, and the wing and fuselage undersurfaces in light blue. The aircraft also carries the yellow markings displayed by all Axis aircraft operating on the eastern front. 'Jozo' Stauder did not score any victories while flying this aircraft type, gaining all 12 of his kills in 1943 with the Bf 109.

2

Bk 534 No 519 (M-8) of catnik Jan Reznak, No 13 Sqn (letka), Spisska Nova Ves, Eastern Slovakia, June 1941

The Bk 534 was the cannon-armed variant of the B 534 (k standing for kanon). Again painted in the standard SVZ camouflage scheme, No 519 was used by future ranking Slovak fighter ace Jan Reznak in his first air combat, on 29 July 1941. He was scrambled in error from Tulczyn to intercept an allied Hungarian CR.42 fighter, Reznak opening fire at too great a range and failing to hit the 'enemy' aircraft.

3

B 534 No 217 (S-18) of zastavnik Frantisek Cyprich, Combined Squadron (Kombinovana letka), Tri Duby, Central Slovakia, August-September 1944

This aircraft was one of four obsolete B 534s operated by the insurgent Combined Squadron based at Tri Duby airfield. It was flown by former members of No 13 Sqn, including Frantisek Cyprich, who had claimed 12 Soviet aircraft shot down. Flying a B 534 during the Slovak uprising against their former German allies, 'Fero' Cyprich shot down a Hungarian Ju 52/3m transport aircraft – the last ever kill to be scored by a biplane with a fixed undercarriage. This aircraft, which displays insurgent markings, is also camouflaged in standard SVZ camouflage colours. The nose is painted yellow, as are the lower wingtips and fuselage band, although the spinner tip is khaki. The aircraft shows considerable signs of wear and part of the cockpit canopy is missing. This B 534 is illustrated displaying the fuselage number S-12, although other sources state that it may have been marked as S-18 or S-13.

4

Bf 109E-3 (Wk-Nr 2945) 'White 2' of catnik Jan Reznak, No 13 Sqn (letka), Piestany, Slovakia, October 1942

The Emil was the first modern fighter aircraft to serve with the SVZ, the Germans supplying more than 20 battle-weary examples in 1942-43. This machine, delivered in July 1942, displays the standard German camouflage of RLM 71 (Dunkelgrün) and RLM 02 (Grau) wing uppersurfaces and fuselage sides and RLM 65 (Hellblau) wing and fuselage undersurfaces. The fuselage sides have also been overpainted with irregular blotches of RLM 71. This aircraft also shows traces of an oversprayed swastika on the tail and a bigger number 2 on the fuselage. In November-December

1942, Reznak flew six combat sorties in this aircraft over the Caucasus, three of which were Ju 52/3m escort missions. The aircraft was also occasionally flown by future ace Pavel Zelenak. After the re-equipment of 13(slow)./JG 52 with Bf 109Fs in early 1943, this machine was repaired and returned to Piestany in April 1943. Here, it was used to train future aces of the second front team, including rotnik Stefan Martis and catnik Rudolf Bozik. The Emil was later assigned to a Readiness Squadron, where it was flown by zastavniks Frantisek Brezina (14 kills), Jozef Stauder (12 kills) and again by Pavel Zelenak, who had by then scored 12 kills.

5

Bf 109E-4 (Wk-Nr 3317) 'White 7' of catnik Stefan Martis, No 13 Sqn (letka), Piestany, Slovakia, October 1942

Another Emil which previously served with the Luftwaffe over Western Europe (with I./JG 52), 'White 7' also displays a similar camouflage scheme (RLM 71/02/65) to 'White 2', seen above. And like the latter machine, this aircraft was also flown by catnik Stefan Martis, who was a No 13 Sqn first and second front team pilot who scored five kills. The Emil survived several crashes, and combat on the eastern front, prior to returning to Slovakia, where it served with No 13 Sqn until 12 April 1944. On this date, whilst being flown on a patrol by zastavnik Frantisek Brezina (14 kills), the aircraft suffered engine failure and the pilot was forced to carry out a belly landing. By then, however, the fighter no longer displayed the number 'White 7' on its fuselage.

6

Bf 109E-7 (Wk-Nr 6474) 'White 12' of porucik Vladimir Krisko, 13(slow)./JG 52, Maikop, Kuban, November 1942

This aircraft was used to train Slovak fighter pilots at Karup-Grøve airfield, in occupied Denmark, and then returned with them to Slovakia. Here, it was marked with Slovak national insignia and the new tactical number 'White 12' in place of the original 95. The first front team emblem was painted on the engine cowling at the same time. This Emil was among the No 13 Sqn aircraft transferred to the eastern front in October 1942, where it was usually flown by deputy CO Vladimir Krisko. He scored the unit's first kill on 28 November 1942, although the victory, over a Polikarpov I-153 north of Tuapse, was never confirmed. The aircraft was also flown by other future aces, including Pavel Zelenak (12 kills) and Jan Reznak (32 kills). It was written-off on 10 January 1943 when it crashed on take-off from Krasnodar with catnik Jozef Vincur at the controls.

7

Bf 109E-7 (Wk-Nr 6476) 'White 6' of catnik Jan Reznak, 13(slow)./JG 52, Maikop, Kuban, November 1942

This Emil was flown from Wiener Neustadt to Slovakia in August 1942 by future 26-kill ace porucik Jan Gerthofer. Once in Slovakia, it received the tactical number 'White 6'. Note that there are still traces of the overpainted German manufacturer's radio call sign (D-IX+WS) on the newly-applied yellow theatre stripe. Sent to the eastern front Wk-Nr 6476 was flown in combat by a number of future aces including

Jan Reznak, who used it to escort Bf 110 fighter-bombers attacking Soviet ground positions on 13 November 1942. On 2 January 1943 the aircraft failed to return after engaging Soviet fighters east of Tuapse, its pilot, rotnik Jozef Drlicka, being shot down and killed. Some sources suggest that Drlicka (who already had one kill to his credit) was actually flying Bf 109F Wk-Nr 8798 on his final mission.

8

Bf 109E-4 'White 1' of zastavnik Frantisek Brezina, No 13 Sqn (letka), Vajnory, Slovakia, September 1943

Worn out Emils performed frontline air defence tasks in Slovakia well into 1944, this particular aircraft belonging to a readiness unit which was later raised to squadron strength. It was then assigned to the air defence of the Slovak capital and the industrial plants in the Povazi Valley. 'White 1' was flown by numerous pilots during this period, including 14-kill eastern front ace Frantisek Brezina. The aircraft displays standard camouflage for this time period, consisting of RLM 74 (Graugrün), RLM 75 (Grauviolet) and RLM 76 (Lichtblau), as well as the mandatory yellow wingtips and fuselage stripe.

9

Bf 109E-4 (Wk-Nr 2787) of rotnik Stefan Ocvirk, Combined Squadron (Kombinovana letka), Tri Duby, Slovakia, October 1944

At the start of the uprising the Combined Squadron was equipped with a motley collection of obsolescent fighters, including Emils which had earlier served on the eastern front with 13(slow)./JG 52. This aircraft was delivered to Slovakia in July 1942 and transferred to the east in October of that same year. It was heavily damaged in a crash landing at Krasnodar on 17 January 1943 whilst being flown by Jan Reznak, the future ranking ace having been attacked by a superior force of LaGG-3s – his fighter had been hit by 60 machine gun rounds and three cannon shells. Following repair, the aircraft was returned to Slovakia in July 1943, where it served with the flying school of the Slovak Air Arms at Tri Duby. When the uprising started, it automatically became part of the Combined Squadron, but due to a shortage of ammunition the fighter was used mainly for reconnaissance flights and leaflet drops. Aside from being flown by Ocvirk (five kills), the Emil was also used by Rudolf Bozik (11 kills and one unconfirmed) amongst numerous other pilots. Insurgent forces set fire to the aircraft on 25 October 1944 so as to prevent it from falling into German hands, then retreated into the mountains. The Bf 109's uppersurfaces were painted in RLM 74 (Graugrün) and RLM 75 (Grauviolet), while the undersurfaces were RLM 76 (Lichtblau). Finally, although the aircraft displayed no tactical number, it still wore Slovak national insignia.

10

Bf 109G-4 (Wk-Nr 19347) 'Yellow 9' of rotnik Jan Reznak, 13(slow)./JG 52, Anapa, Kuban, April-May 1943

This is probably the most famous of all Slovak-flown Gustavs, being used by Jan Reznak to score seven of his 32 confirmed kills during the course of 20 combat missions. Pilots were not assigned particular machines, however, so this aircraft was also flown by other aces, including Vladimir Krisko (nine kills) and Stefan Martis (five kills). The fighter fell into Russian hands when 12-kill ace Anton Matusek defected to the

Soviets on 9 September 1943. The aircraft wore the standard Luftwaffe camouflage scheme of the period, with wing uppersurfaces and upper fuselage sides painted in two shades of grey – RLM 74 (Graugrün) and RLM 75 (Grauviolet). The undersurfaces and sections of the fuselage were sprayed in RLM 76 (Lichtblau), over which irregular blotches of RLM 74, RLM 75 and RLM 02 (Grau) had also been applied. The lower engine cowling, fuselage band and under-wingtips were all marked in yellow in accordance with operational requirements for all Axis aircraft assigned to frontline units in the east.

11

Bf 109G-2/R6 'Yellow 1' of rotnik Izidor Kovarik, 13(slow)./JG 52, Anapa, Kuban, April-May 1943

This Gustav displays standard Luftwaffe camouflage comprising RLM 74/75/76, with yellow fuselage bands and wingtips. Not being Slovak property – they were only 'leased' from the Luftwaffe – the aircraft bore German national insignia. The only indication of the operator's nationality were the white-blue-red Slovak colours on the propeller spinner. Aside from being flown by 29-kill ace 'Izo' Kovarik, 'Yellow 1' was also used by ace Vladimir Krisko.

12

Bf 109G-4 (Wk-Nr 19330) 'Yellow 6' of rotnik Jan Reznak, 13(slow)./JG 52, Anapa, Kuban, April-May 1943

Jan Reznak shot down two LaGG-3s while flying this aircraft, which was fitted with a replacement engine cowling taken from another Bf 109G. Wk-Nr 19330 survived two crash-landings during its service with 13(slow)./JG 52, the aircraft being flown by distinguished pilots on both occasions. On 16 April 1943, deputy squadron CO Jan Gerthofer force-landed the Gustav at Anapa, and on 21 September 1943 it was the turn of Rudolf Palaticky (six kills) to belly the fighter in at Taman. Neither pilot suffered any injuries.

13

Bf 109G-4/R6 CU+PQ of rotnik Frantisek Brezina, 13(slow)./JG 52, Anapa, Kuban, April 1943

This Kanonenboot (gunboat) also wears standard camouflage, RLM 74/75/76, with blotches of RLM 02 on the fuselage and yellow theatre markings. Also noteworthy is the fact that its radio codes (CU+PQ) have not been removed from the fuselage or wing undersurfaces. 'Fero' Brezina claimed the destruction of a Soviet Airacobra on 16 April 1943 whilst flying this machine, although the victory was never officially confirmed.

14

Bf 109G-4 'Yellow 2' of nadporucik Jan Gerthofer, 13(slow)./JG 52, Anapa, Kuban, April 1943

This aircraft wears standard Luftwaffe camouflage (RLM 74/75/76), but with recognisable traces of oversprayed radio codes. Note the unusual spotted engine cowling, the latter obviously having been taken from another aircraft (probably with RLM 02 blotches). The undersurface of the engine cowling is yellow, as are the wingtip undersurfaces and the fuselage band. This aircraft was flown by several pilots during the Kuban campaign, with ace 'Jano' Gerthofer being the most notable.

15

Bf 109G-4/Trop (probably Wk-Nr 15195) 'Yellow 10' of rotnik Stefan Martis, 13(*slow*)./JG 52, Anapa, Kuban, September 1943

Several Slovak aces flew this aircraft during the spring of 1943, including Izidor Kovarik and Stefan 'Pista' Martis. Indeed, Martis pilot crash-landed it upon returning base from a combat mission on 5 September 1943, damaging the fuselage, undercarriage and propeller, but without sustaining personal injury. The aircraft was taken to German field repair shops at Anapa, where it was quickly restored to flying status. Note the dark engine cowling and fuselage, the latter showing telltale traces of the overpainted German radio codes.

16

Bf 109G-4/R6 'Yellow 11' of nadporucik Jan Gerthofer, 13(*slow*)./JG 52, Anapa, Kuban, May 1943

Again displaying standard Luftwaffe camouflage, this aircraft also bears traces of the original overpainted German works radio codes (R?+??). With 13(*slow*)./JG 52 having more pilots than aircraft, this machine was flown by several different personnel. Note that the engine cowling is thickly sprayed with light blotches, and that there are no black fuselage crosses, only the white outline.

17

Bf 109G-4/R6 (Wk-Nr 19543) 'Yellow 12' of nadporucik Vladimir Krisko, 13(*slow*)./JG 52, Anapa, Kuban, April 1943

Krisko was one of the many Slovak aces to fly this aircraft, as was ranking ace Jan Reznak. Its standard camouflage scheme is noteworthy, as are the overpainted German works radio codes.

18

Bf 109G-4/R6 (Wk-Nr 14761) 'Yellow 5' of catnik Rudolf Bozik, 13(*slow*)./JG 52, Anapa, Kuban, September 1943

Rudolf Bozik (with 11 and one shared confirmed kills) distinguished himself not only against the Russians but also a year later against the Germans. He was seriously injured on 26 September 1943 when taking off in this aircraft from Taman on a combat mission. While 'Rudo' Bozik was admitted to Simferopol hospital, the aircraft went to German field repair shops in Taman. Although this *Gustav* looks much like all the others in the unit at the time, it displays an unusual tactical number on its fuselage. The remains of the original German factory codes (??+MS) were also present beneath the wings.

19

Bf 109G-4 (Wk-Nr 14938) 'Yellow 2' of catnik Alexander Geric, 13(*slow*)./JG 52, Anapa, Kuban, September 1943

This was one of three *Gustavs* delivered undamaged to the Russians by defecting Slovak pilots, in this case by Alexander Geric, who claimed nine Soviet aircraft shot down. On 11 September 1943, whilst in combat with a superior force of Soviet Spitfires east of Novorossiysk, he pretended to be hit and landed on the Russian-held airfield of Timashewskaya. Crouched inside the fuselage of the *Gustav* was radio mechanic Vincenc Tkacik.

20

Bf 109G-6 (Wk-Nr 161722) 'White 1' of zastavnik Jozef Stauder, No 13 Sqn (*letka*), Piestany, Slovakia, June 1944

This aircraft was flown by a number of aces, including Gerthofer, Kovarik and 'Jozo' Stauder, following its delivery to Slovakia in January 1944. Wk-Nr 161722 was sent to reinforce the local Slovak Air Arms group in the east of the country in the wake of No 13 Sqn's decimation at the hands USAAF escort fighters on 26 June 1944. On 3 August rotnik Karol Geletko (one kill) crashed the fighter whilst attempting to land at Isla airfield, near Presov, writing 'White 1' off. Like other Readiness Squadron *Gustavs*, this aircraft displays the standard Luftwaffe camouflage scheme, with the uppersurfaces of the wings and fuselage painted in shades of grey – RLM 74 *Graugrün* and RLM 75 *Grauviolet*. The undersurfaces and part of the lower fuselage are light blue (RLM 76 *Lichtblau),* oversprayed with irregular blotches of RLM 74/75/76 and RLM 02 *Grau*. The original German markings were oversprayed in RLM 75 and replaced by the emblem of the Slovak Air Arms and a tactical number in white. Note also the yellow (RLM 04 *Gelb*) fuselage and wing bands. The propeller spinner was probably painted white (RLM 21 *Weiss*) and black-green (RLM 70 *Schwarzgrün*).

21

Bf 109G-6 (Wk-Nr 161720) 'White 3' of nadporucik Juraj Puskar, No 13 Sqn (*letka*), Piestany, Slovakia, June 1944

This *Gustav* was shared by a number of pilots, including Jan Gerthofer and Juraj Puskar, who was killed while flying it on 26 June 1944 when he led eight Bf 109Gs to intercept a heavily-escorted American bomber formation. Six of the Slovakian fighters were destroyed, with three pilots being killed and a fourth seriously wounded. Puskar was overwhelmed by a superior force of Mustangs, and the aircraft, with its mortally wounded pilot still strapped into his seat, crashed near the village of Horne Lovcice.

22

Bf 109G-6 (Wk-Nr 161728) 'White 2' of zastavnik Jozef Stauder, No 13 Sqn (*letka*), Piestany, Slovakia, June 1944

Delivered in January 1944, this aircraft was flown by aces Jan Reznak and Juraj Puskar, as well as Jozef Stauder (12 kills), who became involved in a combat over Slovakia on 26 June 1944 during which the unit was almost annihilated. 'Jozo' Stauder was among the survivors, and although 'White 2' was damaged by American fighters, he belly-landed it in near Ivanka pri Dunaji.

23

Bf 109G-6 (Wk-Nr 161717) 'White 6' of zastavnik Pavel Zelenak, No 13 Sqn (*letka*), Piestany, Slovakia, June 1944

Jan Gerthofer, Izidor Kovarik, Juraj Puskar (five kills) and Frantisek Hanovec (five confirmed kills plus one unconfirmed) were among the Slovakian aces to use this aircraft. Its last flight took place on 26 June 1944, when 12-kill ace Pavel Zelenak was shot down by American Lightning escort fighters. Zelenak succeeded in belly landing near Brunovce, although the badly damaged aircraft was not repaired. Its pilot was admitted to hospital with a broken backbone, and although he remained in the air force after the war, his career as a pilot was over.

24

Bf 109G-6 (Wk-Nr 161713) 'White 10' of rotnik Frantisek Hanovec, No 13 Sqn (*letka*), Piestany, Slovakia, June 1944

With five confirmed kills and one unconfirmed, Frantisek Hanovec was a veteran of all the SVZ's wartime campaigns. He frequently flew this aircraft up until it was written off on 26 June 1944 with Gustav Lang (three kills) at the controls. The latter pilot had just succeeded in destroying a Liberator over southern Slovakia when he was himself shot down by escorting Lightnings. Lang, who was badly wounded, did not attempt to bale out and was killed when the aircraft crashed at Matiloslavov na Ostrove.

25

Bf 109G-6 (Wk-Nr 161735) 'White 8' of zastavnik Izidor Kovarik, No 13 Sqn (*letka*), Piestany, Slovakia, Spring 1944

With 28 kills, Izidor Kovar was the second most successful Slovak ace, and like Jan Gerthofer, he tested this aircraft soon after its delivery to No 13 Sqn. It was, however, most often flown by fellow *letka* 13 pilot Karol Geletko (one kill), who eventually wrote it off in a landing accident at Spisska Nova Ves airfield on 14 June 1944. The fuselage shows distinct traces of the original 'White 8', which is now covered by a yellow band.

26

Bf 109G-6 (Wk-Nr 161742) 'White 7' of rotnik Rudolf Bozik, No 13 Sqn (*letka*), Piestany, Slovakia, June 1944

Following its delivery to No 13 Sqn in January 1944, this aircraft was flown by aces Juraj Puskar, Jan Gerthofer, Jan Reznak and Jozef Stauder, but mainly by Rudolf Bozik (11 confirmed kills and one unconfirmed). On 26 June 1944 Bozik succeeded in damaging a USAAF B-17 Flying Fortress, but 'White 7' was badly damaged in the process and its pilot only just made it back to Piestany. The aircraft was duly repaired, and on 1 August 'Rudo' Bozik flew it to eastern Slovakia to reinforce the Air Arms Group that was providing air cover for Gen Augustin Malar's army corps. Bozik eventually flew it to Soviet-occupied territory on 31 August.

27

Bf 109G-6 (Wk-Nr 161742) ex-'White 7' of rotnik Rudolf Bozik, Combined Squadron (*Kombinovana letka*), Tri Duby, Slovakia, September 1944

Following his defection, Bozik flew this aircraft (in company with Hanovec in Wk-Nr 161725) back to Slovakia to reinforce the insurgent Combined Squadron at Tri Duby, in Central Slovakia. The markings were hastily changed by overspraying the 'White 7' and the Slovak national markings with Czechoslovak khaki, onto which the insurgent insignia was directly applied. During the uprising the aircraft was flown by aces 'Fero' Brezina, 'Vlado' Krisko 'Fero' Hanovec, 'Pista' Ocvirk and 'Fero' Cyprich, although Bozik was its usual pilot. He had shot down nine aircraft while serving with No 13 Sqn, followed by two more confirmed and another unconfirmed as a member of the Combined Squadron. On 6 September 1944 Bozik shared in the destruction of an Fw 189, then claimed a Ju 88 destroyed on the 16th and a second Fw 189 downed on 4 October – all these kills were scored with this aircraft. Cyprich also used it to shoot down a Ju 88 on 12 September.

On 25 October 1944 Tri Duby airfield was surrounded by German troops, forcing Augustin Kubovic (one kill) to flee in the aircraft towards Soviet-held territory. He never made it, however, for the fighter was hit by flak over Dukla Pass and crashed near Hermanovce village, killing the pilot.

28

Bf 109G-6 (Wk-Nr 161725) of stabni rotmistr Frantisek Cyprich, Combined Squadron (*Kombinovana letka*), Tri Duby, Slovakia, September 1944

Another Slovak *Gustav* with a rich history, this G-6 was delivered to Slovakia in February 1944 and flown by Reznak, Kovarik, Brezina and Hanovec. On 1 August the latter pilot took it to eastern Slovakia to reinforce the Air Arms Group, and on the 31st he fled with the fighter to Soviet-occupied territory. Hanovec returned to Tri Duby in Wk-Nr 161725 on 6 September, and literally within minutes of its arrival, the fighter was scrambled (with Frantisek Cyprich at the controls), along with Wk-Nr 161742 (flown by Rudolf Bozik). Both fighters made quick work of a German Fw 189 reconnaissance aircraft. Bozik and Brezina were also among the pilots who flew Wk-Nr 161725 during this period, the fighter eventually being destroyed during a Luftwaffe raid on Tri Duby on 10 September 1944.

29

La-5FN 'White 62' of stabni rotmistr Anton Matusek, 1st Czechoslovak Fighter Air Regiment (1. *ceskoslovensky stihaci letecky pluk*), Zolna and Tri Duby, Slovakia, September 1944

Following his defection to the Soviets on 9 September 1943, 12-kill ace Anton Matusek joined the Czechoslovak air arm the core of which was provided by experienced Czech pilots who had previously served in the RAF. Equipped with Soviet La-5FNs, the regiment participated in the Slovak National Uprising in September-October 1944. Matusek flew 'White 62' from Soviet-occupied territory to Slovakia on 17 September 1944. After Tri Duby was surrounded by the Germans on 25 October he intended to return to Soviet-held territory but was shot down by flak. Crash-landing near Domanovce village, he joined partisan forces and returned to his unit several months later. The fuselage of his fighter is painted in two shades of grey, while the undersurfaces are light blue. The large black outlined '62' represented the two digits of the factory serial number. Note also the dark grey-blue propeller spinner.

30

La-7 (serial number 45210806) 'White 06' of *Gorkovskiy rabochiy*, 2nd Czechoslovak Fighter Air Regiment (2. *ceskoslovensky stihaci letecky pluk*), Prague, May-June 1945

Former Slovak Air Arms aces Frantisek Cyprich, Rudolf Bozik and Stefan Ocvirk served with this regiment, which formed part of the 1st Czechoslovak Mixed Air Division, at the end of war. Some of them flew this aircraft, which was donated by workers at Gorkiy and displays the titling *Gorkovskiy rabochiy*. The aircraft was written-off on 28 July 1946 and subsequently used for structural tests. The coloured spinner and the lightning bolt on the fighter's nose were standard unit identification markings.

31

La-7 (probably serial number 45212611) 'White 11' of rotmistr Stefan Ocvirk, 2nd Air Regiment (*Letecky pluk* 2), Piestany, Slovakia, July 1946

After six years of war fighting under different colours, Slovak airmen returned to the Czechoslovak Air Force soon after VE-Day. 'Pista' Ocvirk (with five kills) had previously served with 13(*slow*)./JG 52, and flew this aircraft shortly after the war. Note that it displays the standard Soviet camouflage scheme, but with Czechoslovak national insignia. The three-coloured propeller spinner and the lightning bolt on the nose were typical of this unit. This aircraft was written-off after a crash on 5 August 1946.

32

B 135 of kapitan Krastyo Atanasov, CO of the Bulgarian Fighter Pilots' School, Dolna Mitropoliya, Bulgaria, 30 March 1944

This was one of four B 135s which intercepted USAAF bombers attacking Sofia on 30 March 1944 after all available frontline Bulgarian fighters had been thrown into the battle, including those from flying schools. In the only combat mission ever performed by the lightly-armed Czech fighter type, Atanasov shared in the destruction of a B-17 with feldfebel Jordan Ferdinanov. Bulgaria ordered 12 B 135s in 1940, which were finally delivered in kit form in 1943. A licence to build the type was also acquired at the same time, but this was abandoned in 1941 and the dozen machines relegated to fighter-training duties upon their arrival in Bulgaria.

33

D.520 'Red 1' of poruchik Assen Kovatchev, CO of the 662nd *Yato*, 2.6 *Orlyak*, Vrazhdebna, Bulgaria, December 1943-January 1944

The Bulgarian air force acquired 96 D.520s following the Germany occupation of Vichy France in November 1942, although none actually reached the country before August 1943. This profile was prepared on the basis of information supplied by the pilot, who was one of the first seven Bulgarian officers to be trained as a fighter pilot in Germany in 1938.

34

D.520 of an unidentified Bulgarian unit, Karlovo, Bulgaria, 1943-44

This D.520 displays a non-standard marking similar to that worn by a Luftwaffe aircraft assigned to a *Geschwader Kommodore* – a position for which there was no real Bulgarian equivalent. The D.520 was highly regarded by Bulgarian fighter pilots, and those flying the type scored 14 confirmed kills during the defence of Sofia. Surviving machines were used as fighter-trainers until 1946.

35

Bf 109E-4 'White 11' of Mikhail Grigorov, CO of the 672nd *Yato*, 3.6 *Orlyak*, Karlovo, Bulgaria, early 1943

This aircraft displays the red devil emblem personally applied to all the aircraft in his unit by Grigorov. It was based on the unit motif of the Luftwaffe's IV./JG 1, but in different colours.

36

Bf-109G-6 'Black 1'of Stoyan Stoyanov, CO of the 682nd *Yato*, 3.6 *Orlyak*, Bozhurishte, Bulgaria, early 1944

This aircraft was flown by Stoyanov until he was promoted to command 3.6 *Orlyak*, after which it was flown by his successor, poruchik Petar Manolev, who supplied the information on which this profile is based.

37

Bf 109G-6 'Red 6' of podporuchik S Marinopolski, 652nd *Yato*, 2.6 *Orlyak*, Vrazhdebna airfield, December 1943

The name (*HELGA*) painted beneath the cockpit of this aircraft is that of the pilot's girlfriend, and the lettering was applied in such a way so that it would look like kill markings from a distance! This scheme was confirmed by Peter Manolev.

38

Bf 109G-2 'Yellow 2'of poruchik Ditmar Spisarevski, 3.6 *Orlyak*, Karlovo, Bulgaria, 20 December 1943

This aircraft was used by Spisarevski to shoot down a USAAF B-24 Liberator on 20 December 1943. Eyewitnesses on both sides say that he then destroyed a second B-24 in a ramming attack, although he was officially credited with just the first victory. This application of this aircraft's individual number in yellow indicates that it is a staff machine.

39

Bf 109G-6 'White 7' of poruchik Somov, Bozhurishte, Bulgaria, Summer 1944

This aircraft was included in the last batch of *Gustavs* supplied by Germany to Bulgaria in mid 1944. Note its late war Erla hood.

BIBLIOGRAPHY

Grigorov, Mikhail, *Burning Sky*

Mlandenov, Alexander, *A Decade of Air Power, Bulgaria 1940-1949. Wings of Fame*, Volume 13

Neulen, Hans Werner, *In the Skies of Europe, Air Forces allied to the Luftwaffe 1939-1945*. The Crowood Press, 2000

Stoyan, Stoyanov, *We defended Sofia*, Articles published in Bulgarian journals *Aerosvyat* (*Air World*) and *Krile* (*Wings*).

OTHER SOURCES

Deltchev, Ivan, (aviation historian and journalist)

Kovatchev, Assen, (former commander, 662nd *Yato*, 2.6 *Orlyak*)

Manolev, Petar, (former commander, 682nd *Yato*, 3.6 *Orlyak*)

INDEX

References to illustrations are shown in **bold**. Plates are shown with page and caption locators in (brackets).